States without Citizens

States without Citizens

Understanding the Islamic Crisis

John W. Jandora

PRAEGER SECURITY INTERNATIONAL
Westport, Connecticut • London

Library of Congress Cataloging-in-Publication Data

Jandora, John Walter.
    States without citizens : understanding the Islamic crisis / John W. Jandora.
        p. cm.
    Includes bibliographical references and index.
    ISBN 978-0-313-35590-5 (alk. paper)
    1. Political culture—Islamic countries. 2. Civil society—Islamic countries. 3.
Islam and politics. 4. Civilization, Islamic. I. Title.
    JQ1852.A58J37 2008
    306.20917'67—dc22   2008008985

British Library Cataloguing in Publication Data is available.

Library of Congress Catalog Card Number: 2008008985
ISBN-13: 978-0-313-35590-5

First published in 2008

Praeger Security International, 88 Post Road West, Westport, CT 06881
An imprint of Greenwood Publishing Group, Inc.
www.praeger.com

Printed in the United States of America

The paper used in this book complies with the
Permanent Paper Standard issued by the National
Information Standards Organization (Z39.48-1984).

10 9 8 7 6 5 4 3 2 1

Copyright Acknowledgment

Appendix by Nawaf Salam is reproduced from "The Emergence of Citizenship
in Islamdom," *Arab Law Quarterly*, ISSN 0268-0556, Vol. 12.2 (1997: 125–147).
Courtesy of Brill.

Contents

Acknowledgments

This book was written at the behest of many people who engaged me in diverse forums: graduate school classes, guest lectures, official conferences, and less formal official meetings. I thank them all for their encouragement, acquaintances and incidental contacts alike. Because of my employment within the defense establishment, one disclaimer is in order. This book was not written in an official capacity and does not represent the official view of any military or public organization.

Because this endeavor was undertaken on personal time, I also thank my wife Gloria for her forbearance in giving up time together while I immersed myself "in another world." Her proficiency with word-processing and graphic design software aided me greatly in preparing this work for publication.

I also commend Nawaf Salam's essay on "Citizenship in Islamdom," which originally appeared in *Arab Law Quarterly*. This article offers further details on the (unfulfilled) quest for citizenship as a motivational ideal in Islamic societies. Because of this, I append it to my own study (by permission of E. J. Brill).

Introduction

It has been several years since the September 11th jihadist terrorist attacks on New York and Washington, DC. The conflict in Iraq has gone through several stages, which the U.S. defense community has struggled to define—insurgency, not insurgency; civil war, not civil war. The Taliban and their allies have been resurgent in Afghanistan. Iran has again chosen to confront the West, the relevant dispute concerning development of nuclear capability. In the West, thousands of pages have been written on the apparently volatile nature of the Islamic world. Such writings attempt to explain the underlying problems or offer solutions. However, I find them for the most part inadequate because they define the "crisis of Islamic society" in terms of an inability to assimilate, or outright antagonism toward, the values and institutions of the West. They likewise define the solution in terms of whether Islamic society can attain democracy. This debate may serve an ideological self-need, but it is logically nonsensical because Islamic society is inherently non-Western, whereas the term *democracy* connotes values and institutions that are inherently Western. The problem with such discourse is that it focuses on "we," our Western measures of worth, rather than on "they." In my view the crisis is due to the inability to recast indigenous institutions and values so as to bring self-assurance to society—to "modernize" from within.

On what experience have I based this position? The experience is partly intellectual and partly practical. For my PhD dissertation, I investigated the early stage of modernization in the Ottoman Arab provinces. It was not my destiny, though, to have an academic career. Even before finishing graduate work, I was employed on a military modernization program in Saudi Arabia and a little later on a joint-venture technology transfer project in the same country. Among many personal rewards, I had the opportunity to work routinely not only with foreign and native Arabs but also with Pakistanis and Somalis. Afterward, I found myself back in the States teaching graduate school as adjunct faculty. My courses on Middle East Area Studies, Politics of Development, and Contemporary Conflict inevitably touched on the crisis and the question of modernization. The course of the conflict in Iraq brought me back to practical endeavors and the opportunity to work with the Maliki government in Baghdad. The daily experiences there were much the same as those I had twenty years earlier in Riyadh. Long-term success is hindered for want of native versions of "public interest" and "civic service."

There is no regret on my part—just frustration at not being able to help my former colleagues. Americans and other Westerners, particularly policy-makers and development-project managers, must have a better understanding of the real problems of "modernizing" or reforming Islamic societies. What is more, the leaders of those societies must make a new effort to revitalize their civilization. Thus, I write to help both sides of the cultural divide, and I hope to stay clear of undue criticism or apologetics. This is the motive that overcomes my reservations, of which I had many. Some Westerners might dismiss this effort as the work of a "nativist" or someone "soft on terrorism." Likewise, some Muslims might dismiss it as another endeavor in "Orientalism." Such reactions seem inevitable, given the harsh feelings on both sides. However, potential adverse audience reaction is of less concern than considerations of scholarly method.

To establish my thesis, I look at the past as well as the present and delve into the topics of cultural borrowing, ethics, hero-lore, and development science—among others. I often use a comparative–contrastive approach, which entails discussion of various subjects from both a Western and Islamic perspective. There exist numerous relevant theories, theses, or reinterpretations for each of these, but it is not feasible to consider them all; thus I omit such dialectic altogether. To compensate, I include many secondary sources, listed by relevant subtopic, in "Further Readings." My text is, by intent, light on footnotes, although I do allow key primary sources to "speak for themselves." I admit that there is some risk in letting Ibn Khaldun "talk" in Chapters 2 and 3. His famous *Prolegomena* (*Introduction to History*) has been the subject of a great many interpretations and commentaries. However, his own words are far more germane to the relevant historical and cultural issues of this study than are the innumerable efforts to assess the coherence of his ideas or to explain the novelty or apparently modern aspect of his thought.

I also acknowledge the hazard of generalization: that is, the derivation of a (general) concept from particular cases. This process amounts to abstraction from actual circumstances and is, in a way, a distortion of reality. Thus, there are inevitably exceptions to a general rule, standard, or model. Such reservations notwithstanding, generalization is necessary to facilitate discussion—to preclude consideration of each and every case. For this study, I rely much on the concept of civilization, which I define as the prominent aspects of culture that are common to several societies. Thus, the term *civilization* contains within it the interrelated concepts of *culture* and *society*. Of the two, society is perhaps the easier one to define. A society is a social grouping with common interests, economy, and culture. This, though, is society at the micro-level. A civilization encompasses several societies, but civilization itself can be equated to a society, albeit at the macro level. Thus, we also speak of society in a larger sense, as in Islamic society or Western society.

As for *culture*, it may be defined as all the knowledge and values shared by a given society. However, that is quite an oversimplification. According to dictionary definitions, culture is the integrated pattern of human thought, belief, behavior, and material production that depends on man's capability to learn and transmit knowledge to succeeding generations. Thus, culture is manifested in customs, myth, literature, history, theological or philosophic thought, "science," art, institutions, and other aspects of human endeavor. Scholars sometimes use the terms *culture* and *civilization* as synonyms. Indeed, such usage parallels the case with *society*. The term *culture* has applicability at both micro (societal) and macro (civilizational) levels.

Upon reflection, it seems almost amazing that America is now turning to culture to understand the current conflict environment. During the heyday of the Cold War, social science was highly preferred as the source of methodology and terminology for the study of conflict issues. The few, bold cultural analyses that surfaced were readily dismissed as "fuzzy thought." However, social science advocates are now conceding the indispensability of cultural analysis to explain human bombs and complex insurgencies. Over the past decade, the American defense establishment has progressed from debating the "Clash of Civilizations" thesis to insisting on the necessity of "Military Cultural Awareness."

The issue of scope, or bounds of the main topic, also warrants consideration. The relevant question: Is it methodologically legitimate to deal with the entire "Islamic world" as an entity? What this term denotes varies according to historical era, not only with respect to geography but also with respect to defining characteristic. The premodern Islamic world was a set of territorial states whose ruling class derived its legitimacy from advocating the faith of Islam. Now, these qualifications are but scarcely applicable. There remains a "Muslim world," but it consists of countries with a Muslim majority population as well as of Muslim minorities in other countries. The present study is restricted to the Muslim majority countries extending from West Africa to South-central Asia to Southeast Asia.

There exist among those countries considerable differences in governmental structure, economy, customs, levels of development, and so forth. Is there an overriding commonality? I believe so: the retention of traditional authority and prerogatives by the religious establishment or unresolved competition between it and advocates of modernization in the arenas of law, public morality, welfare, education, or public services. Such competition is reflected in the terms *Islamist*, *Islamic activist*, or *Islamic modernist*. I make these considerations the basis of delimiting my study. Yet, is it possible to take an all-inclusive perspective of such a vast region? Probably not, because one's range of experience and research is inevitably limited. In this regard, I admit that my own focus is Middle East–centric.

Defining the Islamic world as we have does not, however, resolve all questions regarding the term *Islamic*. We speak of an Islamic world in the present time, but can we still speak of an Islamic civilization? The latter term clearly had relevance in earlier history when it designated a set of societies with common institutions and practices that originated with the guardians of the Qur'anic revelation. Many of those institutions and practices have since been suppressed by modernizing elites or colonial administrators. Indeed, we define the contemporary Islamic world as an arena of competition between the traditional and the modern. Where modern ways have been adopted, regardless of effectiveness, traditional ways no longer prevail. However, the changes and reactions have yet to indicate a trend toward civilizational renewal. So we still speak of Islamic societies and states—if not Islamic civilization—in the present day.

A related problem with the terms *Islam* and *Islamic* is their use to denote both a religion and a civilization, its culture, and its component societies. Some years ago, Marshal Hodgson coined the terms *Islamdom* (noun) and *Islamicate* (adjective) to distinguish the society and its culture from the religion.[1] However, these "unwonted terms," as he himself referred to them, have not been accepted in common usage. Therefore, I use the familiar *Islam/Islamic* but attempt to differentiate meanings by way of context. I trust that this approach will afford sufficient clarity for the reader.

As I establish Islamic society in history as an object of comparison, I must similarly explain my second object of comparison—Western society in history. First, it is necessary to acknowledge the gaps in parallelism. *Western* differs from *Islamic*; the former term is geographic and the latter cultural. The use of *West* and *Western* is actually an arbitrary convention. It might be enlightening to deconstruct that convention, yet I forego the effort lest it overcomplicate my approach. One obvious common factor is that, for the historic range of this study, the *West* also varies in what it denotes with respect to geography and defining characteristic. In the earliest period discussed, the West equates to the late medieval, Latin–Christian societies of western Europe. From the Renaissance to the Age of Revolution, the West denotes the progressive, secular–humanist societies of the same region. In more recent times, the West means the advanced societies of both western Europe and certain of its former colonies, the United States most prominent among them.

As with the term *Islamic,* we speak of the Western world and of Western society as being equal to Western civilization. In this case though, the architects of modern history see historical continuity of civilization, in contrast with the seeming disappearance of Islamic civilization. Another contrast concerns use of the term *state. Islamic state* is currently used; *Western state* is not (except as it applies, albeit in a different sense, to one of the United States). In one sense, state means country. We speak of a Western country, so why not a Western state? The answer to that question derives from the phenomenon of nationalism, which, one should note, is uniquely Western.

Nationalism is the outcome of three developments: an indigenous populace wresting political and economic dominance away from an alien aristocracy; that populace defining itself in ethnocultural terms (language, customs, and so on) as a nation; and the bounding of the state in rough correlation to territory inhabited by said national group. This form of nationalism is characteristic of continental Europe. It is technically called *ethnic nationalism* to differentiate it from the *civic nationalism* of Great Britain and some of its former colonies. However, this distinction is generally unheeded. One consequence of the emergence of nationalism is the concept of the *nation-state*: that is, the ethnic nation and the state being (roughly) coexistent. Thus, Westerners are prone to speak of *nation* as synonymous with *state* and *country.*

The Islamic world did not have this experience, although Turkey came close to replicating it. The term nation-state is non-applicable to that world. Iran, Pakistan, Indonesia, and Nigeria have ethnically mixed populations and may be designated "multinational states." Iraq, Egypt, and Algeria have populations that are subsets of the Arab nation; they may be designated "subnational states." Such ad hoc terms may exaggerate the point; but *nation* does not equate to state or country in the Islamic world. There, nationalism, which was an elusive ideal for the modernizers, has become a subject of derision for the Islamic activists.

Moreover, in certain usage in the West, *state* means something other than country. The differentiation is based on modern sociopolitical theory, particularly that of Max Weber. The state is a political entity with legal status, which includes the set of institutions that have the authority to make rules within territorial bounds and have a monopoly on the legitimate use of physical force. In such theory, the modern state is both separate from and connected to civil society, which consists of the voluntary social organizations and institutions that complement the legitimacy of the state. These institutions are arenas of civic activism, the collective endeavor of public-spirited individual citizens. Society is thus unified by two sets of institutions—apart from the fundamental ones, such as markets and schools. Some scholars contend (and I agree) that this relation is unique to the West. From this perspective, I cast the thesis of the present study in terms of States Without "Citizens."

To offer further perspective on the question of citizenship in Islam, I have included as an appendix Nawaf Salam's article on that topic. This essay traces the conceptual background and the impetus that informed the effort of modern Muslim intellectuals to accommodate the concept of citizenship. It addresses the issue in terms of the tension between contrary ideals and trends of thought, both internal and external to the native culture. Salam's approach, which is legalistic, seems to counter some of my own assertions. However, this disagreement is fundamentally a difference of focus. In his analysis of pertinent concepts, Salam considers (Foucault's) three elements of individualism—awareness of self as both a singular and social being, valuation of private life, and sense of self as field of thought and action. He sees the first as most relevant to citizenship. I opt for the third. Success in linguistically and legally defining citizenship does not inevitably create the virtues of self-responsibility and motivation to improve the conditions of society. From either perspective, the pursuit of citizenship remains "an unfulfilled quest."

The point of all these considerations is to draw attention to the frequent inadequacy of terms and concepts for comparative-contrastive analysis. Indeed, some institutions and practices virtually defy comparison. I have demonstrated the problem with parallel terminology. I should also highlight the problem with equivalence in meaning. Take, for example, the English *martyr*, which is conventionally translated into and from the Arabic *shahîd*. In the Islamic context, a martyr is one who dies fighting for the cause of Islam or the sake of the Muslim community. The act is a matter of honor not only for the deceased but also for his or her extended family, or clan. In the Western context, a martyr is one who suffers or dies for his faith or sacrifices for some principle. The act is a matter of personal merit. Apart from the common aspects of the martyr attaining "salvation" and being an example, the image differs with respect to the person's stance toward adversity (active vs. passive) and the reposing of merit (on relatives too, not just on the individual martyr). Similarly, there can be no truly correct "word-for-word translation" of the concepts *country*, *family*, *virtue*, *science*, *strategy*, and so forth.

In the end, cross-cultural comparison becomes largely contrastive analysis. The process addresses different degrees of the same quality, altogether different qualities, and different combinations of qualities as objects of comparison. Whatever the case, the overall drawback is that people prefer similarity to difference. In conflict situations, as currently exist, difference is often equated with wrongness, vice, or outright evil. Moreover, the attempt to explain difference may be similarly maligned. This tendency to denounce what is different may be more typical of

Americans, given their idealism and sense of morality, than other Westerners. However, Americans have recently shown sensitivity to "cultural diversity" in the domestic environment, and that lesson could be applied to foreign developments.

In consonance with being culturally aware, I am obliged to comment on the transliteration convention (rendering foreign words in English) that I use in this text. In the Middle East and Islamic Studies arenas, scholars have expectations with regard to transliteration and the choosing of Arabic, Farsi, or Turkish variants for common Islamic institutions. As I intend this work for a wider audience, I generally dispense with those conventions. Most personal names and proper nouns are spelled as they would appear in common English usage, without diacritics and long-vowel marking. With a few names I give an alternate, to preclude potential confusion of identity. There is no true solution, though, when the exact same name, correctly (technically) transliterated from Arabic script as Husayn, is commonly rendered as Husain, Husein, Hussain, Hussein, Hosein, or Hoseyn. I do provide the Arabic term, in transcription, for certain institutions and very unfamiliar place names. I also maintain the variant transliteration schemes that appear in direct quotations. As for the variance between Gregorian and Hijri dates, I usually give the date as CE. However, I do cite some Hijri dates where they particularly suit the context. I make these choices in the interest of increasing the readability of the text.

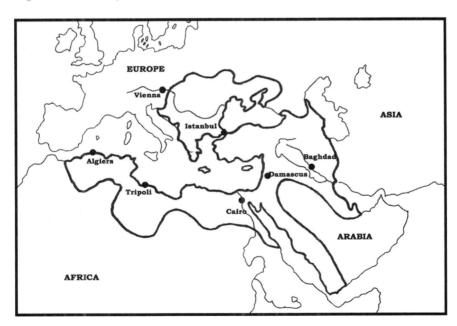

Ottoman Empire, 18th century

HISTORIC SHIFT IN POWER

1500s

Century Trend	The Portuguese attain maritime supremacy in the Indian Ocean region, posing a threat to the southern flank of Islamic world, including Safavid Persia.
1529	The Ottoman siege of Vienna marks furthest advance of sultan's armies.

1600s

Century Trend	The Dutch and British supplant Portuguese dominance in the Indian Ocean region.
1683–1699	"Holy League" victory reverses the trend of Ottoman expansion into Central Europe; the Ottomans cede Hungary and adjoining lands to Austria.

1700s

Century Trend	A relative stalemate exists at the Austrian–Ottoman frontier.
Early–Mid-Century	The British displace Mughal rulers, defeat French rivals, and establish control of India.
1768–1774	The Russo–Turkish War involves Russian naval operations in the eastern Mediterranean; the Ottomans cede territory in southern Ukraine and the Caucasus.
1798	Napoleon's invasion of Egypt further demonstrates the vulnerability of the Islamic heartland.

1800s

Century Trend	The Ottoman regime loses territory (1) in the Danube Basin and the Balkans because of Austrian and Russian advances and Greek, Serb, and Bulgar nationalist movements and (2) in northern Africa because of the foreign occupation of Algeria (France, 1830), Tunisia (France, 1881), and Egypt (Britain, 1882).
Early Decades	In reaction to French and Russian incursions in the Levant, the provincial regime in Egypt and the central Ottoman regime implement Westernization programs for military modernization.
Mid-Century	The Ottoman elites continue efforts to strengthen their state through Westernizing reforms. Russian advances in Turkestan and the Caucasus further constrain the Qajarid Persian and Ottoman spheres of influence.
Later Decades	The Islamic modernist movement originates in reaction to governmental efforts to Westernize (modernize) Islamic society.

1900s

1907	The Anglo–Russian Convention divides Persia (Iran) into spheres of influence.
Early Decades	The Ottoman regime loses further territory in the Balkans and North Africa (Italian occupation of Libya, 1912). Post–World War I treaties lead to the dissolution of the Ottoman state and the emergence of the Turkish Republic; former Ottoman Arab provinces become League of Nations Mandates (Iraq, Palestine, Syria, Iraq).

1

States without "Citizens": Thesis

The Islamic world is in crisis. The heirs of one of the greatest civilizations of history find themselves aliens amid the progress of modernity. Whether seen from within or without, Islamic societies are characterized by relatively low standards of governance, technology, productivity, education, and health. The crisis has continued for generations as efforts to redress it have repeatedly miscarried. Native reformers, looking at internal causes of the malaise, fell short of their aims. Native radicals, looking at external causes, took "center stage" in lashing out at the supposed sources and facilitators of politicoeconomic imperialism. Because of this, the consequences of the crisis have become more problematic for the world community, as is evident in the recent American-led military interventions in Kuwait, Somalia, Afghanistan, and Iraq, as well as the numerous Islamist terrorist strikes in major urban centers across the globe. America has contrived its own solution to the Islamic crisis—instituting the freedoms of democracy.

Some four years into the "war on terror," on June 28, 2005, President George W. Bush gave a public speech at Fort Bragg, North Carolina, honoring American service members at a major U.S. military base and rallying public support for his defense policies. In that address, he distinguished the opposing sides as those who hate freedom and those who love freedom. President Bush used forms of the word "free" over thirty times to argue for staying the course in attempts to bring freedom to Iraq. His speech also included allusions to liberty. Half a year later, on January 31, 2006, the president evoked the same themes in his State of the Union Address, mentioning freedom over fifteen times. America's global mission was made clear: bringing freedom to the oppressed peoples of the world—freedoms of speech, assembly, representation—the characteristic rights of citizens of democratic societies. That message certainly resonated well in those two forums. But how many listeners (or readers) bothered to consider what freedom really means and whether an intervening military force can bestow the rights of citizens where no real concept of free citizenry exists?

Such questioning was unlikely; American educational processes, whether formal or informal, tend to inculcate the belief that all people aspire to American (or Western) political values. The same processes also instill the belief that the ideas of freedom, rights, civil society, constitutionalism, civic duty, and citizenship have equal value and meaning in all societies. But this is overly idealistic and far from representative of the real world. Even in the American experience one generation's civic duty has not always been another's. Conscripted military service was hardly questioned during World War II, but it became a major sociopolitical issue during the Vietnam War.

What, then, of freedom? What qualifies its meaning? Thousands of pages have been written on the subject. Despite—and perhaps because of—this, the meaning of freedom is often taken for granted in public discourse. Freedom is defined as the absence of constraints, whether moral, legal, political, or physical, upon choice or action. In a practical, social sense, however, the word is even more complex. This is apparent in the dictum that freedom is not an absolute good—even in Western society. People are free to pursue their interests to the extent that they do not infringe upon the freedom of others. Freedom is a virtue insofar as free persons balance license with self-constraint. Freedom, then, is an aspect of ethics—a part of the code of correct behavior. Ethics, combined with custom, sustain the personal freedom to decide on political matters without deference to parents, pastors, bosses, or other authorities.

Moreover, freedom is a political symbol. As such, it reflects the conditions that result from the historic compromise between a society and its government. Freedom is a practical admission that free, private enterprise brings more prosperity and power than does governmental direction. So long as such circumstances prevail, freedom remains a key aspect of political culture. In this sense, freedom is the prerequisite of purposeful action. People need freedom to accomplish something—to relocate, to change jobs, to earn a degree, to seek redress for injury, and so forth. Being free to do nothing has negative value for both the development of individuals and the strengthening of society and state. Freedom is a means to an end—not an end in itself. In other words, it is good to be free toward a constructive purpose. In another respect, freedoms (in the plural) amount to the rights formally specified in some constitution; as such, they amount to the benefits of citizenship. Freedom, therefore, makes the most sense in a society that favors private enterprise as the means of achieving the common good, that sets rules for competition, that values individuality, and that encourages active contribution toward the betterment of life.

As noted above, the words "freedom" and "citizen" are closely linked in American—and Western—political discourse. As with freedom, the deeper meaning of citizen cannot be taken for granted. In a general sense, the concept of citizenship has the two elements of reciprocal relation and identity. A citizen is a person who owes allegiance to a state in return for benefits. This relation is sometimes described as "duties versus rights." A citizen is also a person who identifies (or is identified) with the geopolitical entity known as a state or a country. The concept of citizenship, however, shows considerable variance through the course of Western political history. The formal qualifications have varied, as men of affairs sought to differentiate full citizens from other members of society. The image of the citizen has varied as theorists reflected on the key virtue of their times. Aristotle's ideal citizen is prudent, Cicero's is honorable, Augustine's is hopeful of salvation, Machiavelli's is martial, and Locke's is productive.

In its practical aspect, "citizen" is a delimiting term. It differentiates those who are fully members of a given society and state from those who are not. The differentiation may be external (a matter of nationality) or internal (a matter of legal status), although the latter has declined in prominence over time. It is obvious that the citizens of one country do not normally have the rights of citizenship in other countries, but it is perhaps not so obvious that some "citizens" of a state may not have the legal rights of others in the same state. But this was the case in ancient, medieval, and early modern times, when most of the people of a given society were not full citizens. They were excluded for not meeting the qualifications of gender, patrimony, property, length of residence, and free status, (as in the case of slaves). They were required to prove their worthiness of an increased level of citizenship by making sustained contributions to their society and state. In a sense, they earned more rights—or freedoms—by serving the common good.

The intrastate qualifications on citizenship gradually disappeared in the West as a result of the Enlightenment belief that all humans are intrinsically equal (for example, as potential contributors to smaller and larger communities). Today it is unthinkable that any native-born members of the world's advanced societies would not be "full citizens" in a legal sense. This evolution of free citizenship occurred in the West, yet the symbol became universal. It was exported to the non-Western world during the later phases of Western imperialism, in the nineteenth and early twentieth centuries. The former colonies and mandates of Asia and Africa (including most of the Islamic world) are now independent states having their own laws of citizenship. The *symbol* of freedom has been adopted and adapted—but what of the underlying values?

Key among these is proactive contribution to the common good—the betterment of society. This value equates to the self-fulfillment of the citizen, something enabled by freedom under the law—the hallmark of democratic government. The primary point, though, is that preferred conduct is made possible, not caused, by freedom under the law. Were it the reverse, the crisis of Islamic society would likely not exist. Generations of reformers, in official and nonofficial capacities, have commendably endeavored to transplant the governmental and legal institutions of the democratic West. Yet the result has been disappointing. Critics might contend that those efforts were impeded by the persistence of authoritarian ways, but the situation in Iraq disproves their argument. America overthrew an authoritarian regime, ostensibly granting people freedom to contribute to a better society. The reality, however, has been freedom to retaliate: to exact revenge for injuries or injustices. This circumstance suggests that although words and institutions have been invoked, the underlying value system, or ethic, has remained incompatible with the meaning behind the symbols.

This proposition is admittedly contentious in that it defies common Western beliefs about human nature that emerged during the Enlightenment and have become foundational principles of the modern democratic political system: beliefs in (1) inherent equality of all humans, as rational beings, (2) the inalienable rights common to all humans (including freedom), (3) the universal, natural principles of law, and (4) the inevitable progress and perfectibility of society. Staunch proponents of such tenets do not readily accept the suggestion of contrasts in ethics. At the extreme, they even denounce such suggestions as racist—as demeaning of non-Westerners. But acknowledgment of differences between cultures should not be taken as racism. In this discussion there is no implication that the value system of Islamic societies is brutish or underdeveloped. It is different—and being different does not make it bad or wrong. The Islamic value system is the result of a unique history.

But the concept of a unique history is also problematic for those who adhere to the West's post-Enlightenment view of history: the emergence of a world civilization and a global human community. Historic Islamic societies both contributed to and drew from the common civilization (although most of their contributions occurred in premodern times). Many Islamic societies, in fact, have constitutions, elections, and women's suffrage. Some even have female prime ministers. The people of these societies write and converse in ways that are the legacy of Western influence: democracy, rights, and rules of law. So how is their history significantly different? The simple answer is that although they have adopted some of its trappings, they did not themselves invent the precepts and rules behind the social order known as modernity.

A longer answer is that Western societies created their own states, whereas Islamic societies had their states created for them through occupation or pressure by the West. The Western experience was one that featured the interaction of theory and practice: ideas inspiring actions and actions validating ideas. Through dialogue and struggle there arose the justification of secular over ecclesiastic authority, the abstraction of the concept of "state" from dynastic rule, the dominance of the "sons of the land" over the landholding aristocracy, and the setting of bounds on the exercise of authority. These dialogues and struggles were sustained by people who redefined themselves in terms of nationality, civic responsibilities, and legal competence—the elements of citizenship in its modern sense.

But the Islamic experience was of a different kind. The boundaries of Pakistan, for example, were drawn consequent to the dissolution and division of the British colony of India in 1947. The ethnically diverse peoples of various regions became "Pakistanis" overnight, assigned an identity through a linguistic invention that had no connection to any historic place-name. Less blatantly but just as artificially, inhabitants of Amman became "Jordanians," inhabitants of Mosul became "Iraqis," and inhabitants of the Kabylie (Atlas) Mountains became "Algerians." Would those people have adopted such terms of identity if they had actively contributed to the formation of their own states? Amman is situated near— but not in—the Jordan Valley. Mosul is far from the alluvial plain of southern Mesopotamia (Arabic al-ʿIrâq). Inhabitants of a continental mountain range would not instinctively consider themselves to be "of the islands" (Arabic al-Jazâ'ir, linguistically converted into the English "Algeria").

In the case of Turkey, however, reformers within an Islamic society founded a new country much more autonomously. But the ups and downs of their efforts—the reform–reaction interplay—attest to the difficulty of making citizens of subjects. Faced with continuing reversal in the power equation vis-à-vis the modernizing states of Europe, the elite of the Ottoman Empire began seriously considering the need for political (among other) reforms in the early nineteenth century. Consequently, the edict known as the Hatt-ı Şerif of Gülhane of 1839 guaranteed security of life, honor, and property to all subjects. It implicitly invoked certain rights of the citizen, as then known in the West, but did not actually institute citizenship. (That concept would not be incorporated into the Turkish vocabulary until the following century.) More official acts followed that sought to strengthen the allegiance of the populace toward the state. Among the more renowned, the Hatt-ı Hümayun of 1856 specified that all subjects were fully equal under the law—and the Nationality Act of 1869 defined a common collective identity devoid of religious and ethnic qualifications. Despite this effort, contemporary political currents greatly diminished the feasibility of tying the identity of a multi-ethnic, multi-confessional populace to the Turkish-speaking Muslim regime. Those currents eventually led to the abandonment of the Ottoman experiment.

The Ottoman regime's decision to side with Germany and Austria–Hungary in World War I resulted in the permanent loss of Arab provinces and in the temporary military occupation of Istanbul and large swaths of Anatolia. Through a combination of force and diplomacy, nationalist leader Mustafa Kemal (Atatürk) liberated the occupied areas and displaced the Ottoman regime. Consequent to the demise of both dynasty and empire, Atatürk and his colleagues had the opportunity to re-create the state and resolve the issue of nationality. They founded a republic on what remained of the Ottoman domain, and they named that country Túrkiye (in English "Turkey"): the land of the Turk. The term "Turk" may have been pejorative in Ottoman times, denoting certain rural folk. But it served well for the collective identity in the new circumstance, in which the populace consisted mostly of Turkish-speaking Muslims, and the capital was provincially set Ankara.

Resolving the nationality issue helped to solidify allegiance to a new state, but it did not mobilize society in the cause of progress. The leaders of new Turkey saw the need for governmental direction in the absence of a self-enterprising citizenry. Atatürk himself explained that

> Our Republic is very young; it is not capable of contemporary undertakings and all the grand tasks inherited from the past. As in political and intellectual life, in economic undertakings too, it would not be correct to wait for the results of individual initiatives. The significant and grand tasks should be realized in a successful way only by a government . . . relying on all the institutions and power of the state.[1]

However, this statist approach to national development did not forego an effort to create a self-enterprising Turkish citizenry.

In the drive toward modernity and progress, tradition in all its aspects was deemed to be an impediment. Thus, government, working through the Republican People's Party, undertook to divest society of traditional beliefs and practices, the legacy of the late Islamic era. The party-run Turkish Historical Society published writings to convince modern Turks of their ancient legacy of civilization-building—they were the kinsmen and ancestors of the Hittites. The People's Party established networks of Peoples' Houses and Peoples' Rooms that took over many social and informational–educational functions of the traditional rural elite. Such efforts complemented state-initiated reforms in land-holding, personal status and family law, and education, as well as the inaugurations of popular assemblies and constitutions. They weakened tradition with varying degrees of success but could not themselves generate an ethic of active citizenship.

Similar approaches to social mobilization were employed in Persia (later Iran) and the Arab provinces (later successor states) of the Ottoman Empire. Governmental and intellectual leaders pursued the dual track of importing institutions from the modern West while constructing historic links to ancient, pre-Islamic civilizations. Thus the Qajar regime of Persia adopted a constitution in 1909. The successor Pahlavi regime enacted further reforms similar to those of Turkey, styling itself the heir of the Achaemenid rulers of antiquity. The first Pahlavi Shah even changed the name of the country to Iran in 1935 to leverage theories of Aryan migrations ("Iran" and "Aryan" are variants of the same word).

Consequent to nationalist agitation in Egypt, the British terminated their protectorate in 1922, and the Khedive's regime adopted a constitution the following year. By then, the dialogue over modernization and reform in Egypt had been going on for nearly a century. However, the goal of independence inevitably emphasized nationalist thought. A key symbol in the nationalism of that time was Pharaonic Egypt: the vision of an independent country, equal to those in the West, delinked from those in the East, tied to ancient glory. The native experience under the French mandates in the Levant similarly spawned nationalist movements. The French, approving of "Greater Lebanon," allowed that land a constitution in 1926. They disapproved of "Greater Syria," however, and so prorogued the Syrian constitutional assembly of 1928. The Lebanese nationalists claimed a tie to ancient Phoenicia in their construct of collective self-identity.

The civilizations of Hittite Anatolia, Achaemenid Persia, Pharaonic Egypt, and Phoenicia thus became inspirations for new, secular nationalisms. However, these civilizations were known from artifacts of material culture, the subject matter of archaeology. They were not known from records of self-reflection. There was no legacy of thought, as there was in the case of Classical Greece, which speaks on in many philosophic discourses. The pursuits of glorious ancestry mentioned above recovered no lessons in ethics.

In a somewhat different way, the professional and labor associations, political parties, parliaments, and civil codes that were created on Western models were also devoid of an edifying influence. To expect otherwise was over-optimism, for an adopted practice or procedure does not in itself embody an underlying value. Rulers and reformers in new states imported Western institutions to strengthen their societies, but those wider societies did not generate them as the natural expressions (or embodiments) of their own social and political ethics. Constitutionalism in Islamic society, for example, differed from constitutionalism in Western society; very different processes were at work. In the Western world, citizens adopted constitutions to define the concept and capacity of the state. In the Islamic world, states adopted constitutions to define the concept and capacity of the citizen. The words used for "citizen" in the indigenous languages of the Islamic world, unsurprisingly, were all invented in modern times. Loanwords notwithstanding, the state-led approach to modernity failed to meet expectations.

The outcome in the Arab experience is noted by Foud Ajami, who paraphrases the critical views of poet-savant and fellow countryman Khalil Hawi:

> That whole Arab awakening . . . "had covered up the backwardness." The modernists, he said, had not understood the West itself, let alone laid the foundations for a viable Arab renaissance. From distant Western shores these claimants had brought only "those colored empty sea-shells that the tide brings to shore." The society had traded its old forms of backwardness for new ones.[2]

From Iran Jalal Al-e Ahmad laments his country's inability to become modern on its own terms:

> We've not been able to retain our own cultural/historical personality during our encounter with machines and in the face of their inevitable assault. In fact, we've been destroyed . . . as long as we don't perceive the nature and philosophical basis of Western culture, and continue to behave as Westerners superficially, we'll be like the donkey who posed as a lion and ended up being eaten by one.[3]

This testimonial might be extended by hundreds of quotes. But to what avail? It is evident from Western media reporting over the past several decades that something has gone seriously wrong with modernization in the Islamic world. Given the above-noted preeminence of the state, one might question whether the macro-level reforms in the arena of government had been matched by innovations in the arena of civil society. Of relevance here is certain Western political theory which posits that institutions of civil society are essential to democracy. They develop fully participant citizens—people who both can and will contribute to the common good through commercial, communal, cultural, and social activity. The institutions of civil society instill and reinforce the political values that the institutions of state embody. Such thinking was not neglected by the state builders of the modern Islamic world, who imported institutions of civil society along with institutions of government. The modernizers established professional associations, women's clubs, scout troops, sports clubs, and so forth. But these undertakings failed to mobilize the populace as the modernizers had hoped. It may be that some essential conditions were lacking—true "civility" of society (tolerance among groups), and genuine attachment to such institutions. As Augustus Norton aptly observes, without civility "the milieu consists of feuding factions, cliques, and cabals."⁴ The focus of change was apparently off the mark.

The institutions of civil society and state, respectively, emphasize and enforce rules of right conduct. They do not "originate" that which is right or socially good. They are not sources of ethical principles. Rather, ethics emerge from sociopolitical thought as expressed in writings or oral lore, whether in complex or simple messages. The authors of ethics are theorists and professors in scholarly forums as well as storytellers, balladeers, songwriters, humorists, poets, dramatists, literateurs, and journalists in popular forums. The teachers of ethics are parents, other family members, preachers, and instructors in elementary school. Thus, the critical question becomes: How were the authors and teachers of ethics involved in the modernization efforts in Islamic societies, if at all?

There was certainly ample attention given to the necessity for educational reform. As in other arenas, governments led the effort, which largely entailed importing the "science" of the modern West. The ulema (religious scholars) were deprived of their monopoly over education. New-style schools were established alongside traditional ones. Reformers within the government were especially keen on bringing engineering, chemistry, metallurgy, physics, and related subjects into the curricula of higher education. They made a place for teacher education, medical science, and law and became receptive as well to the liberal arts, including comparative literature, world history, and sociology. Officials' desire to maintain state dominance made philosophy, economics, and political science more or less suspect, but they were still found in the offerings of foreign-endowed schools.

The reform effort changed the institutions and substance of education, but not the outcome. It is one thing to teach new subjects; it is quite another to learn them. The ability to focus and comprehend is a key issue. The pursuit of higher studies generally requires a considerable amount of self-discipline: organizing time, completing research, questioning motives and methods, crediting sources, and so forth. However, the value of self-discipline is hard to instill at that level. It should be imparted during a person's formative years through the efforts of parents and schoolteachers. Child rearing, though, remained outside the reach of the modernizers. Reflecting on the ethics of the Arab Levant, Stephen Penrose, once president of the American University of Beirut, commented that "there, discipline is apt to be rigid for the sake of discipline, rather than for the cultivation of intelligent respect for the sound principles of behavior."⁵

Similarly, another American academic who taught in Iran in the early 1960s observed that once the students became accustomed to him, "they lapsed into their usual abominable classroom behavior; whispered, made mischief while fellow students recited . . . studying meant memorizing. . . . As for the term papers, most of the students copied a few paragraphs from encyclopedias or books of criticism; others turned in no paper at all."⁶ Challenges to progress in secondary education were noted by the Shah of Iran himself:

> In the Persian language we have a word *dastan,* which commonly implies something that is neither fact nor fiction but lies somewhere in between. In the past much of our teaching of history and other subjects was in that spirit, and the student learned nothing of modern natural or social science . . . too much of the old *dastan* spirit lingers on even today; furthermore, we still over-emphasize uncritical memorization.⁷

The inclusion of natural science and comparative humanities in the curriculum of higher education is illustrative of the real challenge in educational reform. Learning natural science presupposes acceptance of the scientific method. Comparative study presupposes acceptance of the principle of objectivity. Here again, the familiarization with such principles should begin in the formative years—but apparently does not.

It is one thing to learn new subjects, but it is another altogether to apply such learning, something that requires both opportunity and inspiration. Inspiration falls within the purview of education. Students in Islamic societies might read about the accomplishments of Isaac Newton, Louis Pasteur, Benjamin Franklin, and Cornelius Vanderbilt (among other inventors and entrepreneurs); but they do not generally look to these men as heroes or role models, for such men manifest the virtue ethics of a foreign culture. What, then, of the virtue ethics of Islamic cultures—and the efforts to change them? Such efforts were indeed made, but they were not directed by governments. Rather, they were undertaken by intellectuals and literateurs who worked outside the government, if not in outright opposition to it. The two aspects of that endeavor are starkly manifested in the highly publicized controversy over the book *Satanic Verses.*

On the one hand is Salman Rushdie's extremely sophisticated effort to use a nonnative literary form—the novel—to address the question of what constitutes good and evil. In developing his thesis, he recast the imagery of several traditional "heroes" of Islam—the Archangel Gabriel, or Gibreel (who brought Allah's revelation to the Prophet Muhammad), Sultan Saladin (who led the counter-crusade against the Frankish occupation of the Levantine coastal area), the Prophet's widow Ayesha (who accompanied troops at the Battle of the Camel), and even the prophet Muhammad himself. Such literary invention is a well-accepted Western technique for questioning a society's mores. However, it is too provocative for a society that is not accustomed to social criticism of this kind, as is manifested in the hostile reaction of the Ayatollah Khomeini and other Islamic conservatives.

Khomeini himself played a considerable role in recasting the image of Imam Husayn (Hoseyn), the archetypal hero of Shi'i Islam. The Ayatollah and others who shared a vision for a new Iran faced the task of motivating the populace, which largely accepted its circumstances as they were. The Shi'a of Iran had long revered and emulated Husayn, the slain grandson of the Prophet; but his traditional image was that of a passive victim of tyranny—certainly not an image conducive to the sociopolitical task at hand. Thus the ideologues of the Iranian revolution recast Husayn as an activist martyr who inspired people to abandon passivity and take action—even risk their lives—to change the circumstances of life. This was obviously no lesson in civic virtue as it is understood in the West.

Opinion leaders in Sunni circles who oppose modernization reaffirm the traditional moral code. To rally support, they evoke the traditional hero lore intact. Usama bin Ladin appeals to the deeds of Ja'far ibn Abi Talib, 'Abd al-Rahman ibn 'Awf, and 'Asim ibn Thabit, all of them companions of the Prophet Muhammad and fighters for Islam. The three names are unknown to most Westerners except for a few specialist scholars. Yet Osama alludes to them without a thought for biographic detail, an ease of allusion that suggests that traditional hero lore is still prevalent and meaningful in Islamic societies.

It seems that modernization efforts have replaced institutions but not values. Many Islamic modernists clearly see this shortcoming, but their philosophic endeavor to infuse Western institutions with traditional Islamic values has also fallen short of popular acceptance (as we shall discuss later). This disconnect between reforms and ethics accounts for the disconnect between achievement and aspiration: the ultimate cause of the crisis of Islamic society. To achieve the power of the West, the modernizing reformers sought, whether consciously or unconsciously, to instill the civic virtues of the West: self-denial for the common good, community service, patriotism, industriousness, tolerance in debate of views. Without significant change in the scholarly and popular forums of ethics instruction, the populace of the new states would not be citizens in the Western model. Thus, the world community confronts the phenomenon of "states without citizens." Communal differences are often resolved by violence (Algeria, Sudan, Pakistan, Indonesia), national reconciliations are elusive (Somalia, Lebanon, Iraq, Afghanistan), freethinkers are physically attacked (Egypt, Iran), and loyalties and causes defy state borders.

The last phenomenon is well represented by Usama bin Ladin and his fellow mujahideen. They hail from many countries and operate without regard for borders, touting the merits of a symbolic raid base (al-Qâ'ida) and the necessity of a borderless caliphate. These mujahideen are certainly not acting as citizens of states, but as brothers of oppressed Muslims. Their motive is not national cause or social betterment; it is human redemption and the triumph of their "truth."

These observations evoke the questions that frame the following study: How has history shaped the ethical thought of Islam, in contrast to that of the West? What are the ethical fundamentals of the Islamic social order, in contrast to those of the modern Western social order? What image stands for that of the citizen? What are the prospects for an authentic transformation of Islamic society?

2

Worlds Together, Worlds Apart: Cultures in History

The previous discussion of the crisis of Islamic societies alluded to the reversal of the power balance between the West and the Islamic world, which began in the fourteenth century CE with the Renaissance, Western Europe's intellectual and cultural awakening. As many Muslim reformers and modernists have been keen to point out, the Renaissance was prompted, in part, by contact with Islamic culture. Thus, the perception arises that the Europeans took the learning of the Muslims and made better use of it than the Muslims themselves. In actuality, much of the "Islamic inspiration" for the Renaissance came from Arabic versions of and commentaries on Classical Greek philosophy that had fallen out of use and from esoteric works on metaphysics, astronomy–astrology, and alchemy that had been banned by the Muslim authorities. Islamic society had taken a turn toward conservatism and orthodoxy.

By the early eighth century CE, the first wave of Islamic expansion had run its course. The frontier between Christian Europe and the Islamic dominion was roughly stabilized along an axis extending from northern Spain in the west through the Mediterranean basin to the Taurus range (presently Turkey) in the east. Western Europe, under strong ecclesiastical influence and on the defensive against Muslim raids, was generally not open to intellectual exchanges with the neighboring culture. However, the European intellectual elite eventually divested of this mindset.

The resurgence of commercial activity in the city-states of Italy evoked practical interest in law and governance as secular, not ecclesiastical, matters. This circumstance led to innovation in literature, the humanist movement, wherein writers began to focus on the subject of man in (secular) society—in contrast with man in the "City of God." There also arose opportunities to reflect on pre-Christian and non-Christian sources of wisdom. The launching of the Crusades brought firsthand exposure to the esoteric beliefs and mystic practices of the Levant. The intervening capture of Constantinople by Latin Crusaders gave better access to the Byzantine libraries, which included copies of and commentaries on Classical philosophic works. Such books would gradually be taken to Western Europe as the climate for scholarship in Constantinople worsened over the decades. Meanwhile, a similar corpus of sources, albeit in Arabic, filtered into Western Europe through scholarly exchanges in Sicily and Spain. The recovery of Aristotle's works in particular stimulated interests in both natural sciences and social thought.

Except for the application of Aristotelian logic in theology, Latin Christian Europe had long ignored the works of the famous philosopher. The writings survived, though, through the endeavors of scholars in the Byzantine and Islamic realms. In Constantinople, the works of Classical Antiquity were copied, edited, and interpreted in Greek. In the learned centers of the Levant, they were similarly preserved in both their original and Neo-Platonist renditions, albeit in Syriac as well as Greek. The popular notion that Muslims played the major role in preserving the Classical legacy is, thus, not wholly correct. It derives from later Western historical interest in the large Arabic translation project at the court of the Abbasid Caliph Ma'mun (mid-ninth century CE) and the subsequent careers of the renowned philosophers Ibn Sina (Latin, Avicenna) and Ibn Rushd (Latin, Averroes), who melded Aristotle's original ideas with their own doctrines.

Abu al-Walid Muhammad Ibn Rushd, born in Islamic Spain in 1126 CE, was a great transitional intellectual. He insisted that philosophy was superior to theology as knowledge and so received the acclaim of later Western secularists. In the interim, he was particularly instrumental in stimulating interest in Aristotle among scholars in Europe. Ibn Rushd produced a compendium of summaries and commentaries on most of Aristotle's works (those on natural phenomena plus *Metaphysica*, *Rhetorica*, *Poetica*, and the *Nichomachean Ethics*). Lacking Aristotle's *Politica*, he added a commentary on Plato's *Republic* to the collection. This compendium complemented Latin scholars' efforts to recover and translate Greek copies of the originals. Interest in the pagan Classical wisdom, however, was not readily accepted by the ecclesiastical establishment in Western Europe. The entry of the empiric, naturalist view of Aristotle in company with the more esoteric theories of Neo-Platonists was cause for suspicion and censure. Nonetheless, the translations from Arabic and Greek were avidly read by scientists at the medical school at Salerno and the English philosophers Roger Bacon and Albertus Magnus. Out of that context, there slowly evolved Western "science," scientific reasoning, and applied sciences.

The awareness of new sources of wisdom would influence other arenas of culture as well. Albertus's student Thomas Aquinas partially reconciled Aristotelian thought with Christian doctrine in his *Summa Theologica*—a work that came to represent the apogee of Scholasticism (the pre-Renaissance, normative method of dialectical reasoning) and the essence of Catholic dogma. However, the rediscovery of ancient wisdom had its broadest and most immediate impact in "humanism," which emulated not only the philosophic Greeks but also the noble Romans in literary and academic endeavors.

Humanism is a centuries-old intellectual phenomenon that has taken on different shades in the course of time. It originated as a subcurrent within the European Renaissance. Humanism was not a formal philosophy but rather a mindset and an approach to thinking, writing, and schooling that was influenced by, and, in turn, influenced the study of Classical Greco-Roman writings. The humanist mindset not only infused the Renaissance but stayed vital throughout the Reformation and the Enlightenment into Modernity. The early phase of humanism manifested a number of core principles.[1]

The foundational principle of early humanism was "Classicism," the avid study and use of Classical works—the writings of the Ancient Greeks and Romans—which dealt with the affairs of man in society, in contrast with Medieval Christian writers' preoccupation with spiritual salvation. Familiarity with a range of Classical works was deemed to be both the proper path to personal edification and the proper outcome of formal instruction. In literary endeavor, humanism was expressed as the cultivation of Classical themes and forms. Appreciation and emulation of Classical works inevitably brought some older ideals to new vitality. Hence, the interrelated core principles of humanism might be defined as realism, scrutiny in observation and recording, individual freedom, human dignity, and active virtue.

Realism amounted to taking an empirical approach to knowledge and viewing man in both the physical and social environment. This attention to people and things "as they are" called for critical scrutiny in the study and acceptance of sources and for detail in the capturing of information. Critical scrutiny in turn depended on personal intellectual autonomy, the freedom of the thinking individual to challenge "accepted wisdom." Here was a nucleus for innovation and creativity. Intellectual freedom also implied that people would inquire into their own nature and undertakings. These would be worthy subjects, given that humanity was seen to be dignified, not depraved. With the early humanists, individualism amounted to recognition of personal moral worth. A new mindset created a new kind of wisdom that had an ethical purpose. Yet the wisdom itself did not bring the betterment of mankind; it had to be translated into virtuous action.

The person most responsible for developing this approach to wisdom and promoting it among the intellectuals of Italy was Francesco Petrarca, known as Petrarch, the acclaimed "father of humanism." Petrarch (1304–1374) was born in Arezzo, in Tuscany. At an early age he migrated with his family to Avignon. He studied law—at the insistence of his father—at Montpelier and Bologna, although his real interest was literature. He got the chance to pursue literary endeavors after his father's death. Petrarch returned to Avignon, where he took minor ecclesiastical orders. He entered the service of Bishop Colonna, and that employment afforded him the self-sufficiency and time needed for literary endeavor. At Avignon, he encountered the lady Laura, who became the subject of his famous love poems. About 1330, Petrarch began a period of travels, wherein he wandered through France, Germany, and Italy, sometimes going into seclusion at Vaucluse, near Avignon, to write. During this time he conducted business for Church officials, penned numerous works in verse and prose, recovered neglected manuscripts of Latin literary works of Antiquity, earned fame as a poet and writer, and formed friendships with like minds, such as Boccaccio. In 1353, Petrarch moved away from the environment and politics of Avignon. He spent the rest of his life in northern Italy, where he continued his literary endeavors and occasionally served as an envoy of the rulers of Milan.

Petrarch's views of a new wisdom are manifested in and through his numerous varied compositions as well as in his prolific correspondence, which has been compiled as three collections of letters. He implicitly addressed the active virtue of the Romans in *Africa* and *De viris illustribus*. Yet he acknowledged the dilemma between action and contemplation, promoting the merits of solitude in *De vita solitaria*. He also held that virtue comes from both secular and sacred sources. In *Secretum meum*, Petrarch addressed the struggle of the human spirit by way of dialogues with St. Augustine. He insisted on moral autonomy and promoted self-knowledge as the goal of philosophy, ideas that spawned the humanist value on individualism. All of this effort was unified in his vehement criticism of the method and substance of traditional, scholastic education and his advocacy of his "new studies," *litterae humanae*. He held that literature instills and exhorts virtue, and he exemplified that the poet is a teacher. His literary models were Cicero, Virgil, and Seneca.

Petrarch's influence over his generation derived not only from his prolific literary endeavors but also from his personal example—the energy he exuded and the accolades he received. Among the intellectuals he influenced directly or indirectly was his friend Giovanni Boccaccio, another adept in use of the vernacular. Boccaccio not only expanded on Petrarch's work but made important contributions of his own. His most famous and perhaps most characteristic work was the *Decameron*, a collection of tales about love, which has deeper meaning as a reinterpretation of the human experience based on perceived reality. The younger Coluccio Salutati emulated Petrarch in his writing on morality, debate via correspondence, and recovery of manuscripts. Salutati was an exemplar of the active life and the use of rhetoric for political persuasion; he served as chancellor of the Florentine Republic. Salutati's two successors in the chancellorship were also humanists—Leonardo Bruni was a historian and advocate of humanistic education, whereas Poggio Bracciolini was the foremost collector of manuscripts as well as a moralist, correspondent, historian, and antiquarian. These men of letters collectively made their mark by the mid-fifteenth century.

At that point in history the new intellectual and literary trends were in full stride. The relevant question is whether there was any receptivity to them on the Islamic side of the civilizational frontier. They seemingly did inspire one work, Ibn Khaldun's *Muqaddima* (*Prolegomena*, or *Introduction to History*), which presents a new concept of historiography. It focuses on man in society and offers theories of social change and state formation as a prelude to rethinking the history of the Islamic world. The *Prolegomena* essentially promotes a sociology-like model as the criterion of historical critique.

The approach has been acclaimed in the West, so that Ibn Khaldun is generally credited with being the "father of sociology." Within Western scholarly circles, he has become probably the best known and most cited Muslim intellectual. By comparison, his standing was, until more recent times, less eminent within Islamic circles. Although Ibn Khaldun was not considered to be unconventional, his method of sociological inquiry had no direct legacy there. Ibn Khaldun did not carefully apply his own criterion of criticism in compiling his voluminous World History, *Kitâb al-'Ibar*. Thus, the *Prolegomena* should be re-examined not only to address the anomaly but also to see the cultural state of Islamic civilization. The writing of Ibn Khaldun is as illustrative as that of his near-contemporary, Petrarch.

The stated aim of the *Prolegomena* and its following volumes was to reform the discipline of history to benefit the savants and rulers of the Islamic dominion. That effort entailed a novel approach for the indigenous intellectual culture—the employment of history to edify the ruling class. As Ibn Khaldun himself commented, there existed an "advice for rulers" genre, but his work was not of that kind. Left unsaid is that history in Islamic culture amounted to salvation history—the enfolding of the divine plan for humanity. That could not be the structure for the study of man in his social environment, and hence, Ibn Khaldun sought to introduce a "new science."

The inspiration for that effort, though, is neither cited nor self-evident. One might find it in the author's educational background and career experiences. 'Abd al-Rahman Ibn Muhammad ibn Khaldun (1332–1406 CE) was born in Tunis, the scion of a distinguished family whose ancestors had migrated from Spain a century earlier. He received a conventional Islamic education, which included study of the Qur'an, hadith (corpus of traditions, that is, nonrevelatory sayings and deeds of the Prophet), *fiqh* (jurisprudence), and Arabic grammar and poetry. Yet he also studied and composed works on Sufism and philosophy and interacted with the leading intellectuals of North Africa and Islamic Spain. Ibn Khaldun was exposed to commentaries on Aristotle's thought, which may account for the empiric, categorizing approach of the *Prolegomena*, even though neither the substance of that work nor its interplay of themes is Aristotelian.

Ibn Khaldun's career certainly influenced his motives. He lived in a time of political instability and regime change, and he relocated frequently within the western Islamic world, finally settling in Egypt. He served various rulers in the capacity of courtier, high official, emissary, judge, and professor of jurisprudence. He also spent time in prison and self-seclusion, where he likely dwelt on the basis for—and tenuousness of—political power. However, it was his experience with the Bedouins that evoked the antithetic view of Bedouin life versus urban life. Between 1365 and 1373, Ibn Khaldun organized and led a Bedouin force in the service of one sultan, pacified restive tribes for another sultan, and lived for over three years as the protected "guest" of the Awlâd 'Arîf tribe. He left his haven once he completed the *Prolegomena*—with its distinctive thesis linking Bedouin custom with virtue and virtue with power. Ibn Khaldun's view antedated by centuries the "noble savage" theme of Western thought.

The inspiration for the main thesis seems clear. But what of the secondary themes? These include the need for a new method of historiography with realism as the criterion of credibility, the focus on man in his social condition, the model of change as cycle or pattern, and the concepts of change between generations (forty years) and dynastic lifespan. These themes may well come from the spirit of the times. By the mid-fourteenth century, such themes were already present in the historiographical work of Florentine writers, particularly Giovanni Villani's *Cronica*, which likewise addressed universal history through a local perspective. Although this similarity of ideas has not been thoroughly examined, it is obvious when comparing the writings in question.

In both works the focus on man in his real social condition is reflected in the attention to customs and habits and the detailed surveys of arts, crafts, and commerce. Regarding cyclic change, both works posit four-phase patterns. In the *Cronica*, success leads to pride, pride leads to sin, and sin leads to social decline. In the *Prolegomena*, kin-group solidarity leads to power, power leads to luxury, and luxury leads to social decline—the same outcome. Moreover, both works project the contrast between the virtue of simple living and the corruption of luxury and wealth. Villani wrote the following: "Of such gross customs were then the Florentines, but of good faith, and loyal among themselves and in their state; and in their coarse life and poverty, did more and braver things than are done in our days with more refinement and riches."[2] In a similar vein, Ibn Khaldun wrote: "Sedentary life constitutes the last phase of civilization and the point where it begins to decay. . . . Clearly, the bedouins are closer to being good . . . and braver than sedentary people" who "become used to laziness and ease" (Chapter 6, Sects. 4–5).[3] Aside from the similarities, the main difference in approach is that, for Ibn Khaldun, the nucleus of society and state was the tribe, and for Villani, the city-state.

Ibn Khaldun asserted that he never saw a book like his own. What that meant is not sufficiently clear. In any case, it is certainly plausible that merchants and travelers from Italy brought word of new notions of historiography to North Africa and, hence, to the attention of Ibn Khaldun. Indeed, he mentioned, in an aside, his awareness of the Classicist current in European intellectual circles (Chap. 6, Sect. 18). It also seems that he and Petrarch were "kindred spirits" with regard to their endeavors in autobiography. This observation is not to detract from the genius of Ibn Khaldun or the uniqueness of his synthesis. It points, rather, to the exchange of ideas across the civilizational divide in the Mediterranean region. Ibn Khaldun had some ideas similar to those of Villani, who drew on Dante, who was influenced by Averroes (Ibn Rushd), the great Andalusian commentator on Aristotle. However, evidence for the surge of cross-cultural influence raises the further question as to why humanist thought flourished in Western Europe but was inconsequential for the Islamic world. The answer can be found in various aspects of Ibn Khaldun's composition.

Ibn Khaldun was undoubtedly aware of the risk of provoking the religious and political authorities. Ibn Rushd, who was a study of his, endured banishment and the burning of some of his writings. Ibn al-Khatib, who was Ibn Khaldun's mentor, was charged with heresy and sent to prison, where he was killed. The ulema (religious scholar) establishment, following the teachings of al-Ghazali, had already defined what was knowable and worth knowing through the two divergent means of rational intellectual pursuit and mystical experience. Indeed, an underlying theme of the *Prolegomena* is that dogmatic theology supersedes philosophy when the two disciplines approach a common issue. Ibn Khaldun had to be discreet in getting his message across without upsetting conservative piety and risking censure or worse. Thus, his writing combined advanced philosophic ideas with respect for the conventional piety of the times.

His treatment of prophecy is illustrative (Chap. 1, Sects. 1 and 6; Chap. 6, Sect. 15). Prophethood is a real phenomenon but is not necessary for human existence. Prophets are capable of miracles, and the Qur'an is the greatest of all miracles. The attention to prophecy and the frequent allusion to divine providence respect the norms of traditional salvation history—the unfolding of God's design for mankind. The following reflective remark is a striking testament to divine intervention in history: "Upon close investigation, many instances of what we have said and outlined (concerning the gain or loss of political virtue) will be found among the nations of the past. God 'creates whatever He wishes, and His is the choice'" (Chap. 2, Sect. 19). As for Ibn Khaldun's intended readers, they could accept the role of providence or read deeper into the thesis. In the prevailing social mindset, they were quite probably disinclined to pursue the latter option.

As well, Ibn Khaldun's application of his principles of historiography to the narrative books of the *'Ibar* was inconsistent. He was not particularly rigorous in source criticism. For the near and contemporary events of North Africa, he addressed the function of tribal ethos in state formation. However, for early Islam, he lacked the material for reconstruction, since the tribal histories had long since been assimilated in the context of salvation history. Ibn Khaldun's account seems to be of the same genre as conventionally accepted works with little, if anything, to unsettle established beliefs.

Ibn Khaldun's real originality consisted of his formal theory of tribalism: that is, the normative practice of behaving so as to benefit one's own extended family, or tribal subgroup, as opposed to acting on individual desires. This theory is quite valid, notwithstanding that later Muslim scholars did not reflect on it, the intellectual orientation of Islamic civilization being other than "man in his social environment." Even with the decline of nomadic living over time, Ibn Khaldun's analysis of tribalism remains remarkably apt. The continual significance of *'asabîya* (or kin altruism) is blatantly obvious to anyone who has lived or worked for some time among Arab people.

Yet another factor may account for the destiny of the *Prolegomena*. Over time, the Arabs and Arabized populace of the Islamic dominion were largely displaced as soldier-rulers by Turks—a point that Ibn Khaldun himself emphasizes (Chap. 2, Sect. 27). Thus, Arabic scholarship had little incentive to expand on the implications of Ibn Khaldun's theory, which related tribal power to state formation and dynastic stability. The Ottoman Turks, though, were indeed interested, particularly as they expanded their rule into the tribal world of North Africa and Arabistan. The *Muqaddima* (*Prolegomena*) was studied during the 1500–1600s, partially translated into Turkish during the 1700s, and fully translated in 1863. Outside of Islam, the Europeans, who were becoming imperialistically involved, discovered a kindred mind in Ibn Khaldun. During the 1800s, there appeared several partial translations and one full translation of the *Prolegomena* along with numerous commentaries on its author. Arab intellectuals, too, revisited the writing of Ibn Khaldun (as we will see in Chapter 5).

Lastly, Ibn Khaldun's discourse on the Islamic educational institution tes-
tified to dissuasion from free thought and nonreceptivity to new ideas. In
surveying the crafts (what we would call professions) of Islamic society, Ibn
Khaldun inevitably commented on education—what was taught and how it
was taught. He devoted Chapter 6 to that subject, introducing it by way of a
concise epistemology. Among the key points were that: man is by nature a
social being; wisdom, or knowledge, is necessary to prudent action; knowledge derives from thinking, which entails perception (or sense experience),
introspection, and speculation; culture, in the sense of passing knowledge
from one generation to another, serves to economize the intellectual burdens
of life; and language is necessary for such transmittal. An interesting observation here is that Ibn Khaldun avoided full discussion of the speculative
intellect; the significance becomes apparent later.

Chapter 6 included classification of the "sciences." First were the traditional (what we would call Islamic, or revelation-related) sciences, to
which "there can be no further increases." The unstated reason is that
dogma bans any further reinterpretation of the Prophetic message. The
disciplines include Qur'anic interpretation and reading; prophetic traditions (hadith lore); principles of jurisprudence; jurisprudence and inheritance law; speculative theology (dogmatic and dialectic) and the related
disciplines of dialectic method, source ambiguity, and doctrinal differences; Sufism; and dream interpretation (which is related to the theory of
prophethood). Next were the seven main intellectual sciences: logic, arith-
metic, geometry, astronomy, music, physics, and metaphysics, which
must be clearly distinguished from, and give precedence to, theology.
Medicine and agriculture are subsets of physics. The sciences of language
included grammar, lexicography, composition, and literature, and the latter two concern both poetry and prose.

Ibn Khaldun similarly addressed the various occult disciplines, forms
of magic and sorcery. As most of these were proscribed subjects, he ostensibly included them as advice to his readers. Ibn Khaldun further established a separate subset of "taboo" disciplines, in which he placed
philosophy (in the sense of intellectual speculation), astrology, and
alchemy. He recommended their study only for apologetic purposes, that
is, in defense of orthodoxy, and only after mastery of traditional Islamic
science. In other words, they warranted study only to facilitate refutation
of their tenets. Contrary to the treatment of other disciplines, there was no
classification of the branches and subbranches of the proscribed subject of
philosophy. What Ibn Khaldun actually discredited is the conviction and
teaching that man can attain true wisdom and virtue through mere reasoning. Logic and metaphysics were separately discussed—but mainly to
note that they had been subsumed under theology. Other branches of philosophy were no longer autonomous and hence go unmentioned.
Cosmology and teleology were part of theology, and ethics, as moral code,

was part of jurisprudence. Virtue ethics, rhetoric, and politics were omitted, as they ostensibly had no relevance given the nature of Islamic government.

Ibn Khaldun provided short and long commentaries on the disciplines of knowledge. The subjects were the curriculum of higher education, that is, the subjects that would be taught either at schools or at the classes of private tutors. Regarding primary education, Ibn Khaldun noted some alternative approaches to curriculum but admitted that accepted custom favored the teaching of the Qur'an as the basis of further learning. Regarding educational technique in general, Ibn Khaldun was critical of the reliance on rote learning and cautioned against severity in instructing students—it made them intellectually lazy and induced them to lie and be insincere.

His writing reflected the conventional Muslim belief that human knowledge is a bounded area—all that is knowable and worth knowing is already defined. Ibn Khaldun himself saw the adverse consequence of this—that memorization became the main method of learning. Yet, he agreed with discouraging speculative and innovative thinking insofar as they undermined religious faith. He did not consider that the further consequence for culture overall would be the relative absence of invention.

Indeed, at the time, imagination and inventiveness were being exiled from the public life of Islamic society. This conservative turn was the result of the political consolidation that followed the counter-Crusading efforts of the famous Saladin and the desire of authorities to promote orthodoxy—to preclude the factional and sectarian antagonisms that had previously destabilized society. The historical watershed was the sixth Islamic century (twelfth century CE). In the words of Marshall Hodgson, "There were further experiments in . . . state formation; but unless they fitted in with the new international and Sufi-oriented Sunnism, they seem to have been doomed to futility. Purely locally-oriented sectarian movements scarcely reappeared."[4] "From this point on, Islam presented persistently two faces: one, Shari'ah-minded . . . the other mystical-minded."[5]

Hodgson downplayed the book-burning and intimidation that accompanied this "rehabilitation" of society. Nonetheless, the effort was deliberately undertaken. It succeeded largely because the intellectual and moral justification for it had already been crafted. This justification was found in the masterful works of al-Ghazali (d. 1111 CE), who translated his own crisis of religious conviction into the tenets of what became the new orthodoxy. In addressing the main competing currents of Islamic thought, he called for limiting both speculative theology and speculative philosophy and condemned their combination in radical theosophic and gnostic doctrines, particularly those of the Ismaili Shi'a. He convincingly reconciled religious legalism with mysticism (Sufism). His teaching accommodated conformance in public and nonconformance in private.

With al-Ghazali's compromise, there remained room for the mutation of Sufism. However, in time, Ibn Taymiyya (d. 1328 CE) authoritatively lashed out against its more radical forms.

The institution that sustained and promoted orthodoxy was the *madrasa*—translated as mosque-college, seminary, or (Islamic) law school. This "academy" consisted of a building complex that included religious endowments (*waqf, awqâf*) for the room and board of the students and some teachers, likely a grand mosque, and perhaps a library. Its curriculum was essentially what Ibn Khaldun described in his *Prolegomena*. The Islamic or traditional sciences were the primary studies; the mathematical and linguistic subjects were ancillary courses. Madrasa education ranged from (what we now consider) secondary to baccalaureate and even higher studies. Decisions on administration and hiring of staff were the prerogative of the dignitary who endowed the institution. The founding of madrasas was initially linked to state policy. Sunni dynasts sponsored their construction as one means of consolidating control in the wake of struggles against Crusaders, Ismaili Shi'a, and Mongols. By the time Ibn Khaldun journeyed to Egypt (1382 CE), many madrasas had been established there, as well as in the cities of Syria, Mesopotamia, and Anatolia. Ibn Khaldun himself received appointments at the al-Qamhiyya, al-Zahiriyya, and 'Argatmish madrasas in Cairo.

The product of madrasa education—and of comparable tutoring as well—was the *'âlim* (plural *'ulamâ'*, English ulema), the so-called religious scholar, who would come to perform almost all social functions requiring literacy. In Western terms,

> the Ulema were judges, lawyers, professional witnesses and servants attached to the legal profession and functionary to the state bureaucracy, market inspectors, and supervisors of Waqfs and treasury offices. They were the literate and professional elite of the cities. All realms of public affairs were intrinsic to the duties of this multi-competent, undifferentiated and unspecialized communal elite.[6]

Thus, the influence of the madrasas and their graduates became pervasive in Islamic society and remained so until the educational reforms of modern times. Reform notwithstanding, there has recently been a proliferation of madrasa openings in South Asia. This development should not be interpreted as mass college education, although it does constitute a reversion to traditional means of education.

The fourteenth/eighth century started with strong cross-cultural contacts on the Mediterranean frontier. Nonetheless, there existed two divergent tendencies—one toward free thinking, the other toward dogmatic thinking. That century ended with the "humanities" taking hold in the educational establishment of Western Europe and orthodox theology holding center place in the educational establishment of the Islamic world. Petrarch's "new studies" would spawn the concept of humanism, which has influenced Western sociopolitical thought to the present day. Yet Ibn Khaldun's "new science" found no following among contemporary and next-generation scholars, who saw no need for it. Of course, his new interpretive method was not the only one to be neglected. As Fazlur Rahman remarked, "Orthodoxy had developed an amazing shock-absorbing capacity: all these (innovative) thinkers were held in high esteem by orthodox circles . . . but such statements of theirs as had some radical import were invariably dismissed as 'isolated' (*shâdhdh*) or idiosyncratic and were quietly buried."[7]

From another perspective, the ulema, the intellectuals of Islamic society, were the authors and advocates of Islamic moral and legal codes. They were undoubtedly aware that alternative customary (tribal) laws were practiced openly in rural areas and more circumspectly in urban areas. However, it was not in the interest of their profession to undertake the formal study of such "rules." As for those who enforced and obeyed the rules of custom, their practice was considered to be "private business." It was certainly not the concern of the general public (*al-'umûm* in Arabic), which never had the connotation of fellow citizenry as it did in the West. The divergent destinies of the two civilizations would be seen in their social dynamics and ethics.

The conservative bent in Islamic society is uniquely reflected in the dilemma over *bid'a*—defined as "innovation, a belief or practice for which there is no precedent in the time of the prophet. . . . The objection to *bid'a* has led some Muslims in more recent times to denounce the use of tobacco and coffee, and even of scientific inventions."[8] The gravest consequence is the disinclination to innovate and invent that has long pervaded the Islamic world. Given the ultraconservative stance on *bid'a*, Islamic civilization had no Age of Enlightenment or Industrial Revolution of its own. The living conditions of Muslims have changed in recent history because Westerners uncover oil resources or export canned food, air conditioners, or other conveniences. Muslims use oil revenues and spin-off wealth to purchase the modern inventions of the West. Yet they generally do not invent comparable or better products. The objection to *bid'a* not only stifles modernization but also lends itself to manipulation by anti-Western ideologues.

HISTORICAL TIMELINE

996	Al-Hakim accedes to the Fatimid Caliphate in Cairo and encourages "high culture" of Ismaili (Shi'i) esoteric thought.
1058	Al-Ghazali is born near Mashhad (Iran); his main work defines Islamic orthodoxy through the refutation of speculative theology and speculative philosophy.
1096	Forces from Western Europe launch the First Crusade.

1114	Gerard of Cremona is born in Cremona (Italy); his life's work entails the translation of 87 books from Arabic, including those of highly advanced thinkers such as al-Razi and Ibn al-Haytham.
1126	Ibn Rushd is born at Cordoba (Islamic Spain); his main work interprets Aristotle for the intellectual elite of Islamic society.
1165	Ibn al-'Arabi is born in Murcia (Islamic Spain); he is the last of the great Islamic Neoplatonists, outside of Shi'i Islam.
1171	Saladin displaces Fatimid Caliph, establishes Sunni dominance at Cairo, and initiates purge of Ismaili influences.
1204	The Fourth Crusade captures Constantinople.
1225	Thomas Aquinas is born near Naples (Italy); his main work reconciles Aristotelian logic with Catholic dogma.
1240	Aristotle's *Nichomachean Ethics* becomes available to Latin Europe as a revised, complete translation from Greek manuscripts and adds to the growing corpus of Latin translations of Aristotle's works.
1258	Mongols capture and sack Baghdad, eliminating the Abbasid caliphate.
1263	Ibn Taymiyya is born in Harran (Mesopotamia); his main work condemns heterodox beliefs and practices among Muslims.
1304	Petrarch is born in Tuscany (Italy); his life's work initiates the humanist movement in Europe at the onset of the Renaissance.
1332	Ibn Khaldun is born in Tunis (North Africa); his main work is a new approach to history as the study of man in society.
1469	Niccolo Machiavelli is born near Florence (Italy); his main works concern political theory, and his career spans the peak of the Italian Renaissance.

3

Kinsmen, Not Individuals: Contrast in Ethics

As noted in Chapter 2, Ibn Khaldun wrote during the initial stage of the humanist movement, which occurred on Europe's side of the civilizational divide. Like the early humanists in Florence, he attempted to deal with man in relation to his environment—instead of in relation to divinity and the hereafter. The intellectual task required taking a perspective on civilization, that is, the development of surplus wealth and sophisticated arts and crafts in a sedentary (vs. pastoral) setting. The inevitable question was the same: What is the impetus for civilization? The answer, however, differs. For humanists, it was human enterprise. People make and sustain great cities as centers of state. For Ibn Khaldun, it was regal power. Kings (or sultans) make and sustain great cities as royal capitals.

In the humanists' perception, man was an individual being with the capacity to improve his life, and hence the life of his fellows. That capacity, or potential, is enabled by the inculcation and practice of virtue, which derives from wisdom. Thus, the ideal man is an intellectually autonomous individual. He freely seeks wisdom through study and self-reflection without heed of dogmatic "authority." Some sources of wisdom, though, are of higher worth—such as the Classics. Outside of self, the ideal man is obliged to apply his wisdom toward the betterment of his community. This motive of civic duty, combined with the necessity for individual freedom, leads to the definition and redefinition of citizenship in Western history.

The efforts of the Renaissance humanists uncovered many models of active, civic virtue. The combination of relevant themes is found in the letters of Petrarch, as exemplified in the following extract (italics mine).

> Bear such aid, then, as you can and ought, to your Tribune, or, if that title is extinguished, to your *fellow-citizen*, who *merited well* at the hands of the *Republic*. . . . Your resources are, I confess, no longer what they once were, but never did your fathers show such *valor* as when Roman poverty, which forms the wealth of *virtue*, flourished. . . . If not for the sake of his welfare, dare to *do something* for the sake of your own reputation, *if you still would count* for anything. There is nothing less Roman than fear.[1]
>
> "If you *love virtue* (I address our Charles as *Cicero* addressed Julius Caesar), and thirst for glory—for you will not disdain this thirst, wise as you may be—do not, I beseech you, shun *exertion*."[2]

Leonardo Bruni's rhetoric manifests a similar linkage of themes. "Thus, the only legitimate constitution left is the popular one, in which liberty is real, in which legal equity is the same for all citizens, in which pursuit of the virtues may flourish without suspicion. And when a free people are offered this possibility of attaining offices, it is wonderful how effectively it stimulates the talents of the citizens."[3] Of course, there is debate over the motivations of these "humanists" and the nature of their "citizenship" (elitist vice egalitarian). However, the point here is that their terms of discourse—Classical models, Roman nobility, active citizenship, allegiance to the republic—are unique to, and infuse, Western political thought from their time up to the present.

The same may be said for individualism and literary autonomy. Individualism is reflected in the self-consciousness of Petrarch's autobiographical letters, dialogues with famous Romans, and "secret" confessions to Saint Augustine. As for intellectual autonomy, he decried imitation. "I feared . . . I should imbue myself with his (Dante's) or any other writer's verses, I might perhaps unconsciously and against my will come to be an imitator. In the ardour of youth, this thought filled me with aversion."[4] Bruni similarly scoffed at scholars who were incapable of free-style, rather than literal, translation. (Free-style refers to translating the context, not the word form.) In time, these values would migrate from literary concerns to sociopolitical thought.

Turning to our "other study," Ibn Khaldun, we find a considerably different approach. His concern was the source of regal power, not active virtue as human enterprise. His reflections led him to the concept of *'aṣabîya*, which has been variously translated as *group spirit, cohesion, kin solidarity*, or *kin spirit*. Actually, translation is difficult because Ibn Khaldun used the word in different ways. He struggled for clarity because the technical terminology did not yet exist. The dynamic of *'aṣabîya* is the main topic of Chapter 2 of the *Prolegomena*. Considering the whole context of that chapter, it seems that Ibn Khaldun most often used *'aṣabîya* to mean kin altruism. As he explained, "Compassion and affection for one's blood relations and relatives exist in human nature as something God put into the hearts of men" (Chap. 2, pt. 7). Thus, his thesis took the following shape: The pursuit of easier conditions of living is the motive to exploit power; power is the basis of rule; kin altruism is the basis of power; and proximate contact and interaction among relatives are essential conditions for kin altruism. The development of this line of thought leads to a theory of tribalism, which was Ibn Khaldun's unique, but unheralded, contribution to social philosophy.

Having established the relation of *'aṣabîya* and power, Ibn Khaldun addressed virtue. He inevitably considered it not as a set of ideals for personal behavior but as the enactment of kin altruism. Fortitude and bravery in action are of utmost value because they are essential to survival of the group. Apart from ensuring physical well-being, upholding the honor of the kin group and pressing its claims are also essential. As Ibn Khaldun put it, death in the pursuit of tribal glory is "sweet." Absent from the whole discourse, however, was consideration of the ethics of war-making and the sanction of blood-letting, which would be logical subtopics. Ibn Khaldun further addressed virtue in his discussion of regal authority; he concluded his topical commentary on virtue through discussion of the natural vices of injustice and mutual aggression. In the tribal environment, natural vice is constrained by respect for the tribal shaykhs, that is, the men with experience and wisdom.

The virtue of tribal life contrasts with the vice of the civilized, urban environment. Urban populations have to be constrained by punitive law or educational (social) rules. This is the case because the kinship ethic has been compromised due to the comingling of people and the pursuit of luxury. As Ibn Khaldun contended, people without kin rarely feel affection for their fellows. Urban communities are less virtuous and less courageous because they are accustomed to indulge in worldly desires and ease. Thus, man is a product of his environment, not of his natural disposition. Where religious influence is strong, self-restraint might be inculcated through moral refinement. In any case, law and rules are not true substitutes for the self-restraint that derives from either piety or respect for clan "elders." Two implicit points merit note: the strength of *'aṣabîya* is relative to circumstances and the concept of individualism does not exist.

Of considerable significance is Ibn Khaldun's discussion of the phenomenon we might call notional kinship. He maintained that blood-ties are not essential for kin altruism. The long-term association between a tribe and its clients, and even allies, tends to create the same bonds as common descent. Ibn Khaldun did not address the related process of creating myths of common ancestry. Nonetheless, his observation regarding notional kinship accords with the research of modern anthropologists. He did explain the converse situation, that is, when kinsmen have drifted apart, *'aṣabîya* erodes. The appeal to common genealogy cannot substitute for it when the awareness of kinship exists only in history, nor can false claims to pedigree bring gain to opportunists when they lack the qualities that are essential to high office.

Discussion of bloodline raises the topic of leadership, which Ibn Khaldun saw as a natural function within the kin group. Leadership qualities are passed on in the bloodline. Therefore, status, or prestige, is inherited, and pedigree is essential for claims to status. A lineage of prestigious ancestors constitutes a "noble house." The degree of nobility of lineage correlates with the degree of kin-group spirit because the strength of the kin-group spirit correlates with the avoidance of comingling with other people. The client of a noble family accrues a similar but lesser degree of prestige. For Ibn Khaldun, prestige, like anything in man or nature, must decay. Thus, the rise and decline of a noble house is generally a four-generation phenomenon. The generations were described as "the builder, the one who has personal contact with the builder, the one who relies on tradition, and the destroyer" of the edifice of prestige (Chap. 2, pt. 14).

Regarding the clientage of a ruling noble house (or dynasty), Ibn Khaldun did not elaborate on its other implications. However, in the course of Islamic civilization, it became the norm for rulers to rely on slaves and aliens, that is, clients, to comprise their elite military and guard units or to act as their trusted agents. This practice evolved in reaction to the adverse effect of 'aṣabîya, whereby distrust and active rivalry among indigenous kin groups was prevalent. Thus, for the sake of stability, it became axiomatic to employ nonnatives to keep politically ambitious natives in check. The noteworthy point, in this digression, is the disparity between the Islamic practice and the Western notion of civic, social contract.

Concerning the concept of governing power, Ibn Khaldun explained that regal authority derives from leadership yet differs from it. Leadership is convincing men to follow by appeal to consensus and building trust. Regal authority is commanding men who have committed themselves to obey. It is the outcome of highly successful leadership. The attainment of this situation, though, has consequence only when the tribe is of considerable size or when it expands by way of merger or confederation. In the latter case, kin altruism again becomes an operative factor. The stronger 'aṣabîya absorbs the weaker one, and the new, enlarged tribal organism attains one greater group spirit. This process of expansion continues until the 'aṣabîya confronts another of equal strength and stalemate results. For Ibn Khaldun, regal authority was not only a benefit to society by dint of reason but also an aspect of divine providence.

Ibn Khaldun explained that the qualities of the ruler are the virtues of his kin group. Within the set of virtues, some pertain to any man of honor—generosity, forgiveness of mistakes, care for the poor and weak, fulfillment of obligations, fairness in dealings, and respect toward people (even strangers and rivals) according to their status. Moreover, some pertain to any good Muslim—obedience to religious law and deference to religious scholars, pious men, and teachers. Ibn Khaldun insists that respect of merit in an individual, class, or group is a key virtue—the loss of that quality is the first indicator of a people's decline. Ibn Khaldun did not expound on this point; however, it likely reflects the dynamic of tribalism whereby nonkin may become kin or kinlike through clientage or close association and, conversely, kin or kinlike may become nonkin through intense rivalry and erosion of *'aṣabîya*. The goal is keeping capable people on your side, or at least at your service. Thus, due respect for the merits of others complements the long-term interests of the clan. Of note in Ibn Khaldun's listing of qualities is the nonconsideration of martial vigor, prudence in decision-making, discernment in choosing counsel, or careful management of state resources. Kin altruism, nobleness, and due respect (of "station in life") are the foremost virtues of Ibn Khaldun's ruling elite. These are the "proper" or preferred attitudes toward group survival, equity (or fair treatment), and appreciation of merit.

The antithesis between the virtue of harsh rural life and the vice of sophisticated urban life pervades Chapter 2 of the *Prolegomena*. Ibn Khaldun did not delve into comparative study (of the West) and so conceded nothing on this point. Hence, he was skeptical of Ibn Rushd's assertion that family prestige derived from long-term residence in a city, without recognizing that Ibn Rushd rephrased Aristotle, who focused on the society of the Hellenic city-state. In fact, contrary perspectives inevitably arise from differences between civilizations as to the development of cities. In the Western experience, the city's prosperity depends on the energy and virtue of its citizens, who freely pursue (with respect for law) their economic interests. In the Islamic experience, the city's prosperity depends on the attention of government, which sets the conditions for economic activity. For devotees of Greek philosophy and Roman oratory, including the men of the Renaissance, the city is the arena of active virtue and, hence, superior to the countryside.[5] For Ibn Khaldun, the city is the source of degenerate influences—an environment where law necessarily substitutes for weakened *'aṣabîya* and education serves to tame wild energies, rather than unleash productive ones. For lack of comparative evidence, Ibn Khaldun's new science, *'ilm al-'umrân*, requires a theory of tribalism and precludes a theory of citizenship. In broader perspective, neither concept is addressed in the sociopolitical thought of later Islamic civilization. *Citizenship*, though, eventually becomes a topic in Islamic society's "face-off" with modernization during the nineteenth century.

Ibn Khaldun concludes Chapter 2 with commentary on the Bedouins, that is, camel-breeding nomads, which clarifies that they are not inherently his ideal noble savages. He maintains that they are the furthest from attaining regal authority because of their sense of independence and resistance to government. Their freedom and ease of movement encourage contemptible, not commendable, behavior. They are marauders and looters, who bring destruction to settled life, and their lack of self-restraint can only be remedied through the teachings of a prophet or saint because religious guidance unleashes the positive aspects of *'aṣabîya*. Thus Ibn Khaldun explains the Muslim Arab victories over Persia and Byzantium, which have become faint memories in his time. Ibn Khaldun does not concern himself with the implications of this point; nonetheless, the primacy of religious guidance marks the contemporary and enduring contrast between Islamic and Western sociopolitical thought. In Ibn Khaldun's thesis, human enterprise in itself is inconsequential. In the overall scheme, Islamic history is seen in terms of group dynamism rather than individual prowess, as would be the case in the West.

In articulating his theory of tribalism as the basis of regal authority, Ibn Khaldun inevitably comes to consideration of virtue. His decision to study man as he is in nature ostensibly allows for interpreting an ethic apart from Islamic moralism. Hence, it is instructive to see how Ibn Khaldun's tribal ethics compare with Islamic moral ethics, which the ulema derive from the Qur'an and hadith lore. The three attitudes mentioned previously can serve as the basis of such comparison. Regarding survival—the term may seem strange when spiritual salvation is the objective. However, survival is the way to salvation for the Islamic faith. The historic mission of the Islamic community is to bring all of humanity under a regime of social justice, which amounts to fulfillment of the divine plan. This end state does not require conversion of all of mankind but rather its subjection to a just—that is, Islamic—form of rule. The mission starts with a kin group, or ethnic "nation," as this is the context of the divine–human relation. The Qur'an reads as follows: "Indeed, We sent forth among every nation a Messenger, saying: 'serve you God, and eschew idols.' Then some of them God guided, and some were justly disposed to misguidance" [16:36].[6] "O mankind, We have created you male and female, and appointed you races and tribes, that you may know one another. Surely the noblest among you in the sight of God is the most god-fearing of you" [49:13].

Allah's revelation came in Arabic, via the Prophet Muhammad, to the Quraysh tribal group. Because the respective clans were divided over acceptance of the message, the Prophet created a new family—the *umma*, which would expand as a brotherhood of believers. The Qur'an commends the brotherhood in faith in passages such as the following: "The believers indeed are brothers; so set things right between your two brothers; and fear God; haply, so you will find mercy" [49:10]. "And hold you fast to God's bond, together, and do not scatter; remember God's blessing upon you when you were enemies, and He brought your heart together, so that by His blessing, you became brothers" [3:98]. The brotherhood in faith is notional kinship, and in this sense, Islamic moral ethics reflect kin altruism.

Regarding equity, "social justice" is a prerequisite for salvation, so equity is a pervasive theme of Qur'anic teaching. The revelation is replete with admonitions concerning the treatment of widows, orphans, poor people, petitioners, asylum seekers, and so forth. "True piety is . . . to give of one's substance, however cherished, to kinsmen, and orphans, the needy, the traveller, beggars, and to ransom the slave" [2:177]. To instill correct behavior, Islamic law requires the "poor tax" and makes strict provisions for inheritance. The Muslim who behaves this way is righteous in a moral sense and noble in a social sense.

The quality of appreciating merit in others is likewise part of Qur'anic teaching, although its significance changed as Islamic society became more homogeneous. The early Muslims were first neighbors of and then rulers over Christian and Jewish communities. They benefited from the talents, produce, and crafts of these "others" in pursuit of the divinely ordained cause. Indeed, the Qur'an admonished the Muslims: "Dispute not with the People of the Book save in the fairer manner, except for those of them that do wrong; and say, 'We believe in what has been sent down to us, and what was sent down to you; Our God and your God is one and to Him we have surrendered'" [29:46]. Due to conversions over time, Muslim interaction with other faith groups became relatively inconsequential in the Islamic heartland vis-à-vis the frontier zones. The appreciation of merit became more of the social virtue that Ibn Khaldun mentioned. In any case, hadith lore has asserted that: "The most learned of men is the one who gathers knowledge from others on his own; the most worthy of men is the most knowing and the meanest is the most ignorant." In sum, there appears to be overall consistency between the ethical imperatives in Ibn Khaldun's theory and the traditional moral ethics of Islam. However, the following two issues merit consideration.

Whereas Ibn Khaldun does not address the issue of active virtue, Qur'anic teaching exhorts the believers, collectively, to take action to bring justice to mankind. Examples of numerous relevant injunctions are: to bear witness to the truth of the prophetic message [3:75–76], to be role models for other people [2:143], and to not refrain from fighting injustice [4:75–78]. Further, there is a hadith that discredits going to war for personal motives. Fighting for spoils or fame does not constitute fighting in the way of Allah—the righteous fighter is "only the person who sets foot on the battlefield to raise high the name of Allah."

Another disparity—one of substance—concerns obedience to political authority. Ibn Khaldun's theory and Islamic moral teaching are in agreement that obedience to (political) authority is necessary for social order. The Qur'an commands, "Oh believers, obey God, and obey the Messenger and those in authority among you" [4:62]. However, from that precept, the corollaries diverge. Ibn Khaldun contended that, apart from a religious movement, obedience naturally evolves from confidence in leadership.

Enforced obedience is counterproductive, as it feeds dissent and cannot sustain a regime in the long term. Ibn Khaldun sees apathy toward bad governance as inconsistent with the Qur'an. He actually proposed a model for the successful overthrow of a state—there must exist both a genuine religious reformer and a competent leader of a powerful kin group; the absence of one or the other precludes success. In contrast, within Islamic moral ethics, there was a shift toward unqualified acceptance of authority, which accompanied the turn toward conservatism and orthodoxy. The ulema establishment began to teach that it was better to endure oppressive rule than to initiate strife within the *umma*. This doctrine was justified on numerous traditions of the hadith lore. As Thomas Arnold aptly explained:

> It was not merely the Caliph, but any lawfully constituted authority what-soever, that was to receive the obedience of the subject. . . . The political theory thus enunciated appears to imply that all earthly authority is by divine appointment, the duty of the subjects is to obey, whether the ruler is just or unjust, for responsibility rests with God, and the only satisfaction that the subject can feel is that God will punish the unjust ruler for his wicked deeds, even as he will reward the righteous monarch.[7]

Thus, the following political tenet—authority comes from power; value allocation comes from divine revelation. The contrasting tenet in the West is that authority comes from consent, and value allocation comes from secular law. Beliefs translated into practice reveal similar contrast. In the Islamic experience, the mercantile/manufacturing classes depend on authoritative government to employ its military capability to police the domestic and international arenas; they depend on religion for morality. In the Western experience, the mercantile/manufacturing classes indirectly attain security through representative government; they depend on either public law or religion for morality.

The respective careers of Ibn Khaldun and leading Renaissance humanists illustrate the dichotomy in nontheologic ethical fundamentals between the Islamic world and the West in premodern times. The significance in the difference is the relative emphasis on duty to the kin group versus individual freedom and responsibility. The consequence of the difference is reflected in sociopolitical practice and theory, which authenticate the following paradigms. In the Islamic world, a person's interrelation with state and society is largely a group experience. In the West, a person's interrelation with state and society is largely an individual experience. Thus, in the former case, the concept of self amounts to kinsman or brother, and in the latter, it amounts to citizen.

- Islamic Society
  - The person interacts *indirectly* (via group membership) with the state in the capacity of *kinsman* or "brother."

- That relation is defined as *communalism*—or group-centric identity.
- The key determinant of ethics is *kin altruism*: that is, favoring relatives over self.
- The impulse to right conduct is *kin-group loyalty*.
- Kin-group loyalty in practice amounts to kin-group *exclusiveness*.
- Western Society
  - The person interacts *directly* with the state (as an individual) in the capacity of *citizen*.
  - That relation is defined as *citizenship*.
  - The key determinant of ethics, or right conduct, is *reciprocity*: that is, expecting return of "favors."
  - The impulse to right conduct is *civic virtue*.
  - Civic virtue in practice amounts to *involvement* or civic *activism*.

Such dichotomy risks raising the objection that individuals in Western societies do indeed identify with groups. This is true in that one can be, for example, a scout, a "union man," a parishioner, and so forth. However, the point is that such associations are inherently voluntary. Identifying with a group does not normally affect legal obligations and rights vis-à-vis the state and society at large. Moreover, obligations and rights are the substance of a notional social contract, which is an agreement among individuals.

The paradigm for Western society has been well expressed in countless historical philosophic and literary works, which range from the Renaissance through the Enlightenment to the founding of the American and French Republics. The whole set of terms is found in more or less explicit form in the writings of the leading social contract theorists—Hobbes, Locke, and Rousseau. Civic virtue is a key theme in Bruni's orations, Machiavelli's *Discourse*, and Hume's *Leviathan*. Civic activism gets serious treatment in the writings of Montesquieu, de Tocqueville, and the American founding fathers. As for the interrelated value of individualism—belief in the importance of the individual—it is reflected in works ranging from the *belles lettres* of Petrarch and Montaigne to the socioeconomic theories of Adam Smith and Jeremy Bentham.

Some advocates of Islamic Modernist philosophy would contend that Islamic law does in part accommodate individualism. Comparative study of law uncovers some apparent rationale for their position, in the sense that Islamic family and personal status law, for example, recognizes individuals in the cases of divorce and inheritance.[8] However, the aim of such law is equity within the community, as prescribed by divine revelation—not individual right as deduced from natural law theory. Individual Muslims are brothers in the *umma*, and the interests of the *umma* are safeguarded by government. It would seem then that the "individual and the state . . . are broadly at one in their moral purpose, and so the conception of the individual is not prominent, nor the conception of rights. Islam does not in fact recognize the legal personality of the individual in which his rights are secured to him and vested in him by law."[9]

Most specialist scholars agree that Islam, as both religion and civilization, is highly communitarian—valuing community versus individualism. This concept is manifested in a number of institutions that emerged within the Islamic historical experience. First is the so-called "Constitution of Medina." This charter, drafted by the Prophet Muhammad some time after his emigration from Mecca, sets forth provisions for mutual security and dispute resolution among the communities inhabiting the town of Yathrib (later Medina). The recognized communities are the believers, who are both emigrants (*Muhâjirûn*) and local supporters (*Anṣâr*), native Jewish clans, and native pagan Arab clans. This three-way distinction set forth the terms that endured in semantics but changed in practice in the later political structuring of Islamic society. Believers, of whatever tribal origin, are brothers in the *umma* and, as such, come to be the exclusive, full members of the state. Jews, and also Christians, attain the status of protected communities, with restrictions on participation in state affairs. Pagans are eventually denied inclusion and through successive conquests and conversion become almost extinct inside the Islamic dominion.

The protected status of Jews, Christians, and other People of the Book (that is, of the scriptures) is the institution of *ahl al-dhimma*—roughly "people of obligation"—who are simply called "dhimmis" in English. The "obligation" concerned is the requirement to pay something in return for protection and respect for communal autonomy in custom, law, and internal administration. In earlier times, the payment may have amounted to quartering or provisioning of troops, reporting of information, and other military-related support. However, the payment was most commonly rendered as *jizya*, or "poll tax," which in time became the distinguishing characteristic of dhimmi status. Certain restrictions also came to be associated with that status; for example, dhimmis were banned from riding horses, carrying weapons, or wearing green clothing. These strictures came into force as Islamic society became less accepting of its non-Muslim members. In any case, the status of an individual dhimmi derived "from his membership of a protected community."[10]

The fully developed form of the *dhimma* institution is found in the history of the Ottoman empire. The Ottoman sultanate, as it expanded from western Anatolia into the Balkans and then into the Middle East and North Africa, came to rule over a very diverse population. The sultans facilitated their control by recognizing three communities, Jewish, Orthodox Christian, and non-Orthodox Christian, each of which followed its own internal laws and interacted with the state through a head official. The generic term for such grouping was called *millet*. This division of the populace was based solely on a macro-level distinction of religion. There were considerable differences in language, custom, and doctrine within all three *millets*. These differences were often placated by allowance for local autonomy. They did not become politically significant until the European concept of nationalism began to influence the Ottoman lands during the 1800s.

The *millet* system should not be seen as a scheme of differentiating between first- and second-class citizenship in the Western sense. Dhimmis participated in the ruling establishment in the capacity of bureaucrats, advisors, or court physicians. Muslims who were not in the ruling (*askeri, miri*) class were considered to be in the subject (*reaya*) class. However, when the issues of nationality and citizenship became critical, they were not be resolved by the Ottoman regime—as various subject peoples went their own ways. In the final days of the sultanate, "Turk" meant "Muslim" and "Greek" meant "Christian." So, Kurds in Anatolia involuntarily became Turks, and Turcophone Christians in Thrace involuntarily became Greeks. Whether taken from a legalist or sociologic viewpoint, the Islamic experience did not recognize a direct relation between the individual and the state.

To accommodate the theological moralist perspective, we might recast the previous paradigm for Islamic society as follows.

- The person interacts with the state in a manner that is qualified by faith-group membership, in the capacity of "brother."
- That relation is still defined as communalism in the sense of faith group–centric identity.
- The key determinant of ethics is faith-group altruism.
- The impulse to right conduct is the quest for human salvation.
- The quest for human salvation in practice amounts to greater and lesser jihad—respectively, the cultivation of personal morals and the effort of bringing all mankind within the dominion of Qur'anic social justice.

One cannot say that the one civilization is wholly communitarian and the other is individualistic. Yet, there is a clear differential emphasis on kin (and faith-group) altruism in Islamic society versus reciprocity in Western society. Islamic moral teaching emphasizes macro-level kinship (brothers within the *umma*), although that message was suppressed in the practical societal emphasis on micro-level kinship—brothers by common parentage or notional common descent. Western ethics emphasizes reciprocity—the rights and duties of individual members of society.

The aforementioned ethics and institutions were the cultural inheritance of the early modernizers in Islamic society. This was the matter they had to remold, if they dared. There was no alternate source of wisdom and virtue. Their search for it in the ancient civilizations of the Near East was futile; the artifacts did not speak. They could not imitate the men of the Renaissance, who had long since appropriated the symbol of the Hellenic academy with the political philosophy that it forged as well as the symbol of the Roman Senate with the orations that resounded within it. Models of individualist civic virtue would not resonate in the society of brethren and kinsmen.

The divergent path of the two civilizations is also reflected in governmental practice. In this respect, Ibn Khaldun's model for attainment of regal power and his insight on *aṣabîya* remain remarkably valid in the present time. Among others, David Pryce-Jones confirmed this point as he surveyed the careers of rulers in modern-day Middle East and North Africa. He found the following commonality:

> The most successful challenger is obviously he who works his way through the elimination of every rival and seizes the supreme prize of the state. In form, his career starts like that of any civilian. Rising upon the energy of his ambition, he must seek to bind together a retinue of men on whose services he can rely, in all likelihood kinsmen or friends and associates since childhood. Then comes another circle of those connected by village or tribe.[11]

4

Mujahideen and Hero-Martyrs: Imagery of Active Virtue

The impact of Western modernity on Islamic society evoked various reactive trends, among which were modernization, Islamic modernism, and Islamic activism. Modernization has been equated with Westernization, the importing of ideas and institutions from the West. Its proponents could not reasonably promote the heroes and role models of the West, who were not present in the popular historic consciousness. They might have commemorated the philosopher–scientists of medieval Islam, such as Ibn al-Haytham, except that the ideas and books of these men had been denounced by the orthodox. Moreover, they were not prepared to explain how, for example, alchemy gave rise to chemistry. Atatürk became a hero to the modernization movement as a whole; but his persona was far beyond emulation by common people.

Islamic modernism sought a rationalistic approach to revitalize Islamic values. The philosopher–scientists of old were rationalists, too, but the substance of their thought disqualified them as role models for the general populace. Besides, being inherently intellectualist, the movement was not in search of activist heroes. When both modernization and Islamic modernism proved unconvincing, Islamic activism filled the void and exploited an extensive "archive" of traditional hero and martyr lore. As with any advanced culture, this archive consisted of formal biographies and biographic histories, elementary-school lessons, and folk legends. In the American experience, for example, multiple genres commemorate the deeds of George Washington and Benjamin Franklin.

As for the theme of active (Islamic) virtue, it was generated in the writings of Abul A'la Maududi in British India/Pakistan, Sayyid Qutb in Egypt, and Ayatollah Khomeini in Iran and in exile. The similarity in their

approach is reflected in the following quotes, which attest to the importance of ideals and role models.

"The ultimate aim of all the prophets' missions . . . to regiment all such
people who have accepted Islamic ideals and moulded their lives after the
Islamic pattern with a view to struggling for power and seizing it by the
use of all available means and equipment. . . . Muhammad's mission was
carried on successfully by two great leaders (Maududi)."[1]

"It is this spirit (social justice) which dictates the very high standard
required by Islam as the objective to which its adherent must strive and
seek. . . . Such a spirit it was which influenced . . . the spirits of heroes,
sending them forth as a living wave of powerful armies, in the deeps of
which all personal values and all events and circumstances were sub-
merged (Qutb)."[2]

"It is our duty to preserve Islam. . . . It is for the sake of fulfilling this
duty that blood must sometimes be shed. There is no blood more precious
than that of Imam Husayn, yet it was shed for the sake of Islam, because
of the precious nature of Islam. (Khomeini)."[3]

In the morality and ethics of Islamic society, mankind gains salvation
as a group, and it gains honor as a group. If the pursuit of either endeavor
presents hindrance, then the brother or the kinsman is expected to
retrieve the situation, even face challenges that might be fatal. The act of
dying in combat for the sake of either the community of believers or the
kin group has great merit in the indigenous mindset. Thus, the culture
legitimizes and promotes such pursuit of salvation and honor by numerous means. The exhortations of contemporary political leaders, preachers,
and propagandists have been publicized in the Western media coverage
of the theocratic Iranian regime, the Palestinians, and the "global
jihadist–terrorists." However, there are cultural forms that are less publicized, if at all, that instill the tendency in people to dedicate—even
sacrifice—themselves for a higher purpose. Ample images, themes, and
models are found in both tribal and Islamic hero lore.

The hero lore of Islamic culture consists of oral legends and historio-
graphic narratives concerning the Prophet, the Companions of the Prophet,
certain of the Prophet's relatives, and the Muslims who led the conquest
movement, the great jihads and counter-Crusades, and the cross-border
raiding at the Islamic frontiers. The Prophet obviously stands in a class of
his own. Of the very long list of other names, perhaps the only one familiar
to the West is Saladin (Salah al-Din); even his notoriety derives mainly from
his interaction with the Crusaders. The limits of Western awareness
notwithstanding, the virtue of Muslim heroes, and particularly the manner
of its commemoration, has great significance for modern-day "activists" in
many parts of the Islamic world.

Who, then were the Companions of the Prophet? A definite list cannot
be attained, as the history of their time is ambiguous; however, the

approximate number expands well into the hundreds. One can readily get some idea of "Companion" lore through an Internet query on the terms "Sahaba" or "Companion(s) of the Prophet." These are the people—mostly men and a few women—who had direct contact with the Prophet Muhammad and made active efforts to support his mission. They are commemorated primarily for dedication to the cause of Islam, and their personal valor or active virtue is promoted as model behavior. Any one of these worthies might be selected for emulation depending on the edifying purpose at hand. Thus, the fighters who die for Islam become the role models of present-day combatants. For example, Palestinian resistance slogans recall the martyrdom of Khubayb al-Ansari, and Usama bin Ladin's "Declaration of Jihad" recalls the death in combat of 'Asim ibn Thabit al-Ansari.

The circumstances of the deaths of the two hero-martyrs are recorded as follows. Khubayb was captured by hostile pagan tribesmen who over-whelmed his small patrol in the action commemorated as the encounter (day) at Raji'. He was sold to the sons of a Meccan man whom he had killed in the earlier battle of Badr, and they were keen to exact revenge. Khubayb was a model prisoner, but he was dismembered and crucified. His dying words were, "I am being martyred as a Muslim, do not mind how I am killed, for my death is for Allah's sake."[4] As for 'Asim ibn Thabit, he was the leader of the Muslim patrol engaged at Raji'. He fought to his death rather than surrender to pagans.

Within a decade of the deaths of Khubayb and 'Asim, the Muslim Arabs penetrated the frontier defenses of the Byzantine and Sassanid–Persian empires and initiated the great Islamic conquest move-ment, which rapidly extended to the Pyrenees in the west and Central Asia in the east. (This is the same "movement" that Arab nationalists and Arabists are prone to call the "Great Arab Conquests.") Many of the believers who participated in those campaigns have been commemorated in both Islamic salvation history and tribal lore. However, it is the record of salvation history that pertains here. Allah granted victory over the imposing forces of two empires, and the Muslim warriors and their com-manders were his instruments. Of the latter, the most famous is surely Khalid ibn al-Walid, who led many successful expeditions—in Arabia (including Yemen), the Sassanid Euphrates frontier, and Roman Syria. He held "field-command" in the great victories over the Byzantine Romans at Ajnadayn and the Yarmuk. Thus, he is renowned as the "Sword of Allah." He is first and foremost an instrument of divine providence and second-arily a military genius. His persona in itself does not merit study; Muslim historians virtually ignore his tactical methods and are not even sure when or where he died.

Islamic culture reflects debate over who is the second most famous of the conquest leaders. However, the "majority vote" would probably go to

Sa'd ibn Abi Waqqas, the "Archer of Islam," because he commanded at the first major Muslim victory over the Sassanid Persians at al-Qadisiyya. There are many other commanders who might be commemorated, depending on the context of "Islamic conquest"—Egypt, North Africa, the Maghrib, and Spain to the west, and upper Mesopotamia, the Iranian lands, Central Asia, and Sindh to the north and east. As for Sa'd, he represents Allah's victory over the Persians, as Khalid does over the Byzantine Romans. Both men were Companions of the Prophet; however, they have the added distinction of being military commanders in major campaigns. Khalid is renowned for victories over the Byzantines in Syria-Palestine, thus, he is included in the hero lore of the Palestinian resistance. Sa'd, like 'Asim ibn Thabit, is mentioned in Bin Ladin's "Declaration of Jihad."

The historic necessity for the rulers of the Islamic dominion to drive back foreign adversaries offers further examples of heroism in the cause of Islam. The related symbols of *jihâd*, war against infidels, and *mujâhid*, one who conducts jihad, became especially prominent. The public in the West has recently become familiar with both—the latter in its popularly rendered plural form *mujahideen* (from Arabic *mujâhidîn*)—primarily due to media coverage of the "war on terror." That same public is also unknowingly familiar with two of the great figures of jihad lore, Harun al-Rashid (alternately, Rasheed), by association with the tales of "the Thousand and One Nights," and Saladin, as the noble antagonist of the Crusaders, particularly after the 2005 movie "Kingdom of Heaven." Islamic history offers a quite different perspective on these men.

Harun was the fourth caliph of the Abbasid dynasty, who directed numerous military campaigns against the Byzantines in Anatolia. He became renowned for his quick and compelling military action against the emperor Nicephorus, who had peremptorily abrogated an existing treaty between the caliphate and the empire. Saladin attained exceptional renown as unifier of the Islamic domain and organizer of the counter-Crusade. He began his career as an officer serving the Atabeg Nurredin but soon seized an opportunity to become the de facto ruler of Egypt. From that base, he marched to dispossess a number of local Muslim sovereigns in Syria–Palestine, defeated the Crusaders at the Horns of Hattin, and recovered Jerusalem (in 1187 CE). His later endeavors involved the purge of Ismaili Shi'i cultural and political influence from Egypt and dependent lands and the building of many Sunni madrasas.

Saladin's popularity in Islamic society has overshadowed that of Sultan Baybars, who brought completion to Saladin's earlier endeavors. Baybars evicted the last of the Crusaders from the Levantine coastal cities, sustained pressure on the Ismaili extremists, and checked the Mongol invaders at Ayn Jalut in Syria. Outside of formal history, Baybars, Mamluk Sultan of Egypt, became the hero of a popular saga (or romance) in which he contended against the various enemies of Sunni Islam. His commemoration in oral lore has, however, diminished with the spread of modern entertainment media. Contemporary jihadists are more likely to allude to the symbol of Ayn Jalut as an event rather than the image of Baybars as a war-leader.

Among the most famous mujahideen there is a particular subset known as *ghazis*—border raiders. This distinction was relevant where the Islamic dominion abutted with Byzantine–Christian territory on one frontier and Hindustan on another. As the Ottoman Turks eventually led the military effort against the Byzantine state and the Balkan kingdoms, their beys and fighters constitute a significant class of heroes within Turkish folklore. With Turkey pursuing peaceful policies in the present time, there is virtually no reason for ideologues to recall the heroism of the ghazis, but their stories remain intact, nonetheless. In the east, the situation is different. Pakistan is at odds with India, the Kashmir conflict has raged for decades, and Afghan mujahideen have fought the forces of two (infidel) superpowers. In this area, the story of Sultan Mahmud of Ghazna has particular significance.

In Anatolia, the ghazi ethos developed from a situation of military stalemate and consequent change in the military society of the borderland. The unsuccessful Arab-led siege of Constantinople in 716–717 CE was a historic turning point for Muslim penetrations into Byzantine territory. The struggle between the caliphate and the empire subsequently evolved into a pattern of raid and counterraid as the Muslims initially pushed westward, temporarily lost considerable ground, and finally pushed on again. The ethnic composition of the Muslim frontier forces became increasingly Turkic, and the Arabic ghazi lore was adopted by the Turks. In legend, the Arab 'Abdallah al-Battâl became Sayyid Battal—the ancestor of the Turkish ghazis. Over many decades, semi-independent warlords (*beys*) carried out the frontier raid activity (*ghazâ*) as a popularly and officially acknowledged form of jihad. By the early fourteenth century CE, Osman Ghazi, the eponymous ancestor of the Ottoman dynasty, had became one of the most prominent frontier war leaders. Legend made Osman and his fighters the exemplars of the ghazi image—"lacking pride in the world" and "striving in the path of Allah."[5] This image was the heritage of his successors. In later history, the Ottoman sultans "attached the greatest importance to safeguarding and strengthening the reputation which they enjoyed as ghâzîs in the Muslim world."[6] Even with the end of the Ottoman dynasty, Mustafa Kemal was acclaimed as "Ghazi."

Although the legend of Osman Bey had significance for Ottoman legitimacy, it has no such ideological value in modern Turkey. In contrast, the legend of Mahmud of Ghazna resonates in the present conflicts in South Asia. In history, Mahmud was the son of a high-ranking Turkic slave-soldier whose troop-command at Ghazna (in present-day Afghanistan) became the means of de facto independence. Mahmud, who displaced his brother and succeeded his father (in 997 or 998 CE), was intent on establishing the legitimacy and Sunni credentials of the regime. He undertook campaigns against the Shi'a of Khurasan (eastern Iran) and the infidels of northern India. He became especially famous for launching seventeen raids into India, destroying temples, and taking valuable loot and prisoners. Mahmud used his increasing wealth to transform Ghazna into a center of Perso–Islamic culture. For his earlier efforts, the Abbasid Caliph bestowed on him honorific titles; he himself assumed the title of ghazi. In the present day, Mahmud is commemorated in the national history of Afghanistan and Pakistan as a great mujahid and sponsor of culture and is also honored by Kashmiris and other indigenous Muslims of India. Conversely, he is demonized by Hindu nationalists. In a similar vein, Usama bin Ladin is referred to as a ghazi in both favorable and unfavorable contexts.

The preceding discussion is not quite the whole picture, for among the Shi'a, the relatives of the Prophet also have particular prominence as heroes of Islam. 'Ali ibn Abi Talib, the Prophet's cousin and son-in-law, is held to be a model of virtue, even by many Sunnis. Indeed, he is the fourth and last of the "rightly guided" caliphs. He is renowned for his piety, nobleness of character, and intelligence, as well as for his valor in war. 'Ali reportedly participated in all the major campaigns of the Prophet's time, with the exception of Tabuk. Known as Haydar (lion), he was a skilled swordsman and slew many enemies of Islam in combat, his "duels" at Badr and Khaybar being among his most famous. His virtue notwithstanding, 'Ali faced repeated challenges to his right to be caliph. He fought the battles of "the Camel," Ṣiffîn, and Nahrawân against other Muslims who opposed his rule. In the end, he was assassinated and ultimately became the figure of "man betrayed" in Shi'i lore.

'Ali's son Husayn (Hoseyn), grandson of the Prophet, holds at least equal reverence among the Shi'a. His early life was not the active story that his father's was, but he, too, encountered betrayal and became the paragon of the martyrdom of the just. Husayn's "ordeal" began when dissidents in Kufa encouraged him to claim the caliphate, which had passed from his father to the Umayyad clan in Damascus. He traveled from Mecca toward Kufa with family members and a squadron-size escort (70 or so, according to tradition), only to find his welcome retracted. The entourage encamped near the city for a respite but found itself surrounded by a large Umayyad force sent by the Caliph Yazid. The "blockade" extended for ten days, as Husayn remained valorous, refused to succumb to oppression, and denounced Yazid as a heretic. In the end, the Umayyad soldiers massacred Husayn and his escort and brought back severed heads and captives to Damascus. Husayn's sacrifice brought no immediate political change, but it led to great reverence for the "Lord of Martyrs." His ordeal and death on the 10th of Muharram are commemorated annually as 'Ashura.

The accounts of 'Ali and his son Husayn are an attempt to summarize information that has filled hundreds of pages in many versions and perspectives. Thus, there exists abundant material for use in motivating active virtue. It is beyond this study to compare the many renditions; however, the relevant point is that these two heroic figures are commemorated frequently in so many non-literary ways that they are "alive" in present-day Shi'i society. Such commemoration consists of murals at cemeteries, "street-theater" performances with costumes of the period, and processions. The features of the processions include drum beating, flagellation and other ritual self-punishment, the spraying of rose water, and the parading of paintings, standards, and cradle-biers.

The above-mentioned heroic lore, both Sunni and Shi'i, serves the edification of society, and particularly the young. That process, however, requires interpretation—the correlation of the historic or mythic images to presently important values and behavioral norms. Such interpretation is provided informally by parents and adult relatives and formally by elementary school teachers. The former situation is, by its nature, difficult to catalog. However, the latter situation can be gleaned through study of school programs and textbook content. Elementary school curriculum in much of the Islamic world manifests the use of hero lore to inspire and mobilize society in the cause of vital interests.

Let us consider first Pakistan, whose existence as a modern country was determined through consideration of religious demographics. When Britain terminated its colonial rule over the Indian subcontinent in 1947, the Muslim and Hindu nationalists had already decided to go their separate ways. Provinces were aligned on the basis of religious majority and contiguity of territory, and Muslim-dominant Pakistan and Hindu-dominant India came into being as new states. The separation was not without considerable violence and loss of life, which contributed to a lingering distrust. Thus, Pakistan attained self-identity as an Islamic state and a frontier (or ghazi) society, facing the far more populous, infidel state of India. Pakistan upheld that image through support to persistent insurgency in Muslim-majority Kashmir, three wars with India, numerous mobilizations, and competition in developing nuclear weapons. The Soviet intervention in neighboring Afghanistan added a second dimension to confrontation with the infidel world as Pakistan supported the Afghan mujahideen resistance by various direct and indirect means.

Consistent with this historical experience and the consequent importance of the military establishment, elementary school "textbooks contain: (1) all the military heroes, (2) narrations of the specific battles in which the heroes had fought, (3) narrations of the glorious victories from Islamic history, and (4) poems urging jehad."[7] The themes of the texts further promote jihad and martyrdom in the following ways: learning objectives include awareness of the blessings of jihad and recognizing its importance in life, the concept of desire for jihad, and the activity of making speeches on jihad and martyrdom. The heroes of the textbooks range from modern-day Pakistani officers and rankers, who were highly decorated for their deeds, to Khalid ibn al-Walid and Sa'd ibn Abi Waqqas of the early Islamic conquests.

Guidelines for the development of curriculum reflect the names of heroes of intervening times. In local history there is Muhammad ibn Qasim, who led Muslim forces in the conquest of Sindh and the Punjab; Mahmud of Ghazna; and Tipu Sultan, who resisted the British takeover of Islamic India. From general Islamic history are drawn Nurredin Zangi and the more famous Saladin, both of whom fought the Crusaders. Of particular significance for the young are the names Mu'adh and Mu'awwadh, two adolescent fighters who killed Abu Jahl, arch-enemy of Islam, at the Battle of Badr. Additionally, a higher-level supplementary text lauds Shihabuddin Muhammad Ghuri, who supplanted the Ghaznavid sultans and resumed raids against Hindustan; Babur, who founded the Mughal dynasty through military exploits; and Aurangzeb, who pushed the borders of the Mughal empire to their furthest extent. These warrior-rulers are, respectively, models of justice and loyalty, humaneness, and faith and courage.[8] The mujahid theme is not exclusive, however, for the curriculum also addresses the character traits and deeds of the founders of the Islamic *umma* (the Prophet, his family, his Companions, and his immediate successors) as well as the founders of modern Pakistan. Of further note, school texts are complemented by the commercial publication of juvenile literature on heroism, such as the Heroes of Islam Series authored by Fazl Ahmad.

In neighboring Iran there is a comparable educational agenda. Since the fall of the Shah, Iran has been promoting its self-image as the guardian of Shi'i Islam and the hub of the Islamic Revolution. Surveys of Iranian curriculum indicate that it complements that policy and inculcates the values of martyrdom, reinterpreted as activist self-sacrifice, and jihad.[9] The main historic heroes of the textbooks are inevitably Imam Husayn, the "Lord of Martyrs," and his father Imam 'Ali, "the perfect human being." However, hero status is also accorded to other members of the Prophet's family, the later imams, the righteous ulema, and even to non-Shi'i Muslims who died for Islam. Contemporary heroes include Khomeini and his colleagues among the ayatollahs, who actively condemned the Shah's regime. The story of Husayn Fahmideh, "the Mobilized Teenager" who sacrificed himself during the Iran–Iraq War, is also prominent. In the laudatory words of Ayatollah Khomeini, "Our leader is that boy of thirteen years who took a grenade with him and lay beneath a tank."[10]

The textbooks' pictorial representations of the martyr motif include an illustration of Imam Husayn's death at Karbala, with a complementary drawing of children mourning him on 'Ashura, as well as pictures of the shrines of the martyr imams at Najaf ('Ali), Karbala (Husayn), and Mashhad (Reza). The importance of jihad is likewise conveyed in the schoolbooks. For example, one lesson states that the prayer leader holds a gun during his sermon to show that an Islamic society is always prepared to fight for the faith. However, the jihad theme has a variant that is not militant, and the martyrdom theme has a variant that does not involve death. To promote the value of cooperation and its two aspects of contribution and dedication, elementary texts discuss the "*jehâd-e sazandeg*—that is, the regime's endeavor to mobilize the public for renovating the cities and particularly the villages of Iran."[11] As for martyrdom, the same texts teach that mere readiness to sacrifice oneself for one's fellow is the highest level of *ithâr*, the virtue of giving preference to others.

The textbook lessons are complemented with programs that are directed by the Ministry of Education. At the appropriate dates, the schools commemorate the martyrdom of Imams 'Ali and Husayn through mourning ceremonies and ritual re-enactments. They also show edifying videos, which during the Iran–Iraq War included footage of troops at the front. Similarly, in class, students are encouraged to discuss their Noruz (New Year) ritual, which entails visiting nearby families of martyrs—that is, war dead—as priority to visiting one's own extended family.

As with Pakistan and Iran, the Palestinian Authority (quasi-state) has had to inspire society to strive against adversity. That effort is reflected in the elementary-school curriculum for both the lower and higher grades, which raises questions regarding the fate of people whose land has been conquered and occupied. The lesson of history is that the Muslims' treatment of subject people in the older era of the Islamic conquests contrasts with the European and Zionist treatment of Arabs in the newer era of imperialist-colonialism. Another significant point is that the early conquests are depicted as reactive moves, and thus defensive jihad—which links them to the great campaigns against the Crusaders and Mongols, and then to anti-colonialist revolts. The "roll call" of heroes thus includes not only Khalid ibn al-Walid and Salah al-Din but also figures of more recent renown. Seif Da'na reported that in twelfth grade texts, "the stories told are those of Abd al-Qader of Algeria, Omar al-Mukhtar of Libya, Iz ad-Din al-Kassam and Abd al-Kader al-Husseini of Palestine."[12] The deeds of these men reveal the anti-colonialist theme of the lessons.

'Abd al-Qadir al-Jaza'iri, who was a religious scholar and notable, inherited the leadership of resistance to the French two years after they occupied Algeria (in 1830). He mobilized and led tribal and Sufi militias in three separate jihads before he was finally compelled to surrender in 1847. 'Umar al-Mukhtar, who was a member of the Senussi (moderate Sufi) order, led a nearly twenty-year guerrilla warfare effort, as jihad, against the Italian forces occupying Libya (since 1912). He was eventually captured and executed, thus gaining the status of martyr. 'Izz al-Din al-Qassam, a Syrian teacher and mosque imam, supported the resistance in Libya and later in his homeland (against French occupation). He had to flee Syria and so went to British Palestine. There, he established the Black Hand organization in 1930 and led it in anti-British and anti-Zionist activity until he was killed by British police in 1935. 'Abd al-Qadir al-Husayni (Husseini) was a member of the prominent Husayni clan of Jerusalem. Amid the three-way antagonism in British Palestine, he organized a clandestine self-defense group and later led militias during the "Arab Revolt" of 1936–1939. He went into exile in 1938 but returned to Palestine and died fighting in the war of 1948.

The last two men are well known outside of formal instruction. The Hamas organization has chosen the name 'Izz al-Din al-Qassam to designate the "brigades" that constitute its military wing. The actions of those units are well publicized through various means, and such publicity serves to equate the namesake with active resistance. 'Abd al-Qadir al-Husayni is quite famous as a native hero, and his name is inevitably mentioned in discussions of the 1948 war. A street in Gaza City has been named for him. The messages of the streets, and of the camps, have high significance not only in Palestine but also in other Islamic societies experiencing duress.

In 1979, two events disrupted the stability of Southwest Asia—the Iranian Revolution and the Soviet intervention in Afghanistan. One common consequence was the display of a quite non-modern form of militarism. In Iran, revolution replaced the Shah's regime with Khomeini's Islamic Republic, whose propaganda soon brought on war with Iraq. The ill-prepared Tehran regime eventually fought to a stalemate, mainly through reliance on human wave attacks by Revolutionary Guards and Basij militias, which caused large numbers of Iranian fatalities. The will to sacrifice was sustained by a multifaceted program that promoted jihad and martyrdom for a sacred cause. As noted previously, Khomeini and his colleagues recast the traditional image of Imam Husayn into a motif of activist self-sacrifice. That new value was inculcated in Iranian society through many means. Thus, Ayatollah Khomeini exhorted the populace in his 1983 Muharram speech, recalling that Hoseyn gave permission to his son "to go to the battlefield," so may the Creator "cause us to be among the people of Karbala."[13]

The government's program emphasized the commemoration of martyrs (war-dead) through the dedication of special graveyards in large and small cemeteries. These "gardens of martyrs" were decorated with banners, signs, and posters, which included quotations from the Qur'an and speeches of Khomeini and other leaders and also artwork depicting soldiers fighting, women and children mourning the loss of loved ones, and martyrs praying for salvation. Inside these grounds, families set up personal memorials. These often consisted of glass display cases holding photos of the deceased in both military service and younger life, accounts of death in battle, and various personal items, such as letters, plastic flowers, or prayer beads.

Kamran Aghaie summarized:

> [M]emorials of martyrdom also emerged in other forms. . . . Symbols of struggle and martyrdom also became center pieces of *meydans*, or squares at major intersections. Special newspaper and magazine articles and radio and television programs memorialized the sacrifices of the fallen martyrs. Streets, parks, schools, mosques, and other sites were routinely named after martyrs. For the families of martyrs and those wounded in the war . . . foundations were also created. There were also religious gatherings devoted specifically to honoring the families of martyrs.[14]

A similar yet different form of popular militarism evolved as a consequence of the Soviet intervention in Afghanistan. The resistance forces led by traditional tribal and religious elites claimed the honorific title of "mujahideen." They became symbols of heroic active virtue, not only locally but also internationally. Their exploits were first publicized in the world's news media and later in journals and various genres of books in diverse languages. The mujahideen attracted acclaim and moral and materiel support from the Islamic world, which decried the encroachment of infidels, and from the Western Bloc as well, which needed to hinder its rival. They became heroes even in the American press and the "Beltway"—the euphemistic home of the U.S. government, affiliated think tanks, and lobbyist agencies. Among those who ventured to join the native mujahideen were hundreds of volunteers from many parts of the Muslim world and a small number of "adventurers" from the West.

The "true measure" of the mujahideen mystique is, however, seen in the unfolding of events. After the withdrawal of the Soviets and the overthrow of the puppet regime, the resistance alliance fragmented, and the militia leaders turned against each other. The resulting struggles left the populace exposed to further miseries and injustices at the hands of warlords and criminals, and a new movement, the Taliban, emerged to save society in the Pushtun south. The Taliban launched a new jihad, which eventually became an effort to impose Islamic governance on the whole country. Their initial rapid success evoked wonder, but it did not have the same strategic import as the earlier resistance to the Soviet Union. The Taliban might have prevailed were it not for Mullah Omar's unshakeable partnership with Usama bin Ladin, which brought on confrontation with the United States.

That confrontation led to two interesting developments for the topic of heroism. First, the term *mujahideen* reversed its connotation among observers in the United States and allied countries. Many of the native and "Afghan Arab" mujahideen who had fought the Soviets had joined or allied with the Taliban. Thus, in the American perspective, they had gone from being friends to enemies. Once synonymous with heroes or freedom fighters, *mujahideen* became, in Western usage, synonymous with villains and extremists. Nonetheless, the meaning within the Islamic world did not change. Moreover, as our second point of interest, the Taliban leadership was able to survive the U.S.-led intervention and recently revitalized its militant efforts against the Kabul regime and its foreign supporters. The new "recruits" ostensibly follow the model of the nameless heroes who fought in so many past actions. They may be inspired by words such as Bin Ladin's appeal: "We exhort our Muslim brothers in Pakistan to fight with all their might. . . . I bring you the good news that we are established on the path of *jihad* for God, following God's Prophet, with the Afghan people, who are heroes and believers."[15]

Across Pakistan's northeast frontier, the long-running insurgency in Kashmir cultivated the same image of heroism. Indian General Arjun Ray, who once led the counter-insurgency effort, has recorded the efforts of the local and Pakistani media to promote the jihad theme. Apart from television and radio programs, propagandists distributed video tapes of the funerals of martyrs. At the spring 1995 confrontation at the Tsrar-e Sharif Shrine, the fighter Mast Gul ostensibly became the favorite of the jihadist media. His picture was "everywhere . . . AK 47 in hand, the left forefingers raised in victory sign . . . pontificating on his being ordered by Allah to slay the infidels and restore Islam."[16] General Ray was not impressed with the actual deeds of Mast Gul, but he knew that the media image of him was quite advantageous to the insurgent cause.

The decade that began with Iran pursuing war with Iraq and Afghani mujahideen battling Soviet troops ended with a Palestinian uprising (intifada) in the Israeli-Occupied Territories. This third struggle was similarly sustained by vivid appeals to undertake jihad and, later, self-sacrifice for the cause. The previous survey demonstrates the existence of ample material that might be reconstructed by activist oppositionists and their leaders. Indeed, such material was found in the formal statements of Hamas founder Sheikh Yasin, who adopted the ideas of Sayyid Qutb and 'Abdallah 'Azzam, the mentor of Usama bin Ladin. It was also found in informally crafted "messages of the streets." This second kind of media consisted of songs, poems, sketch-art, graffiti, banners, posters, and mosaic-like panels as well as jihadist videos, makeshift martyr shrines, and martyr photos, cards, and calendars. (Thus, the Palestinians created a subculture similar to that of Iran's hero lore, albeit without state-level backing.) Such material is not the normal fare of academia; however, Anne Marie Oliver and Paul Steinberg have masterfully compiled a very readable "catalogue" of the hero lore of the Palestinian intifada.

The following examples are typical of a vast array of the hero lore of the streets. An art panel contains the sketch of an "Islamic ninja," who is "dressed typically, in Islamic green and poses with an M-16 and Qur'an. Hanging from his belt are his knife and a grenade . . . beneath him lie the skulls and bones of the dead."[17] Children parade in the street as they leave school, singing the following:

> Oh mother, my religion has called me to jihad and self-sacrifice
> Oh mother, I am marching toward immortality; I will never retreat.

Various posters contain the words:

> At your service, Islam of heroism. All of us will sacrifice ourselves for you. Hattin: Salah wrote it, so don't you see that we will celebrate our Hattin with the destruction of the Jews.

The words of Khubayb al-Ansari—"do not mind how I am killed, for my death is for Allah's sake"—are cited in graffiti, in song, and in the Hamas anthem.

The commemoration of current-day martyrs is likewise taken up in the media of the streets. A poster commemorating the death of two Fatah activists, trainer and trainee, presents a "roll-call" of martyrs, passing on to "the hunted Anwar Suleih, for whose sake his cub, the hero Tahsin Abu Shama, sacrificed himself."[18] Martyr videos demonstrate that self-sacrifice is a response to the call of truth and that full commitment to Islam must precede combat.

> I charge them, insha'Allah, before they pick up a rifle, to carry 'aqîda (Islamic creed) in their hearts, as well as faith, for if they carry Islam and 'aqîda in their hearts, they will be able to carry the rifle. Islam and faith without 'aqîda and without action do not exist.[19]

The slogans of the resistance and the last words of the dying also accord special honor to the mother of the martyr (*umm shahîd*). People come for weeks to the home of the martyr to honor and support the family.

This ethos may seem similar to Nathan Hale's famous saying, "I regret that I have but one life to give for my country." Actually, it differs in that the element of civic patriotism is missing, as is the element of civic duty. There is no pledge among the mujahideen of Iran, Afghanistan, and Palestine to promote general welfare or to support and defend some constitution. These warriors seek salvation in the afterlife or honor for their kin group or faith community in the present one. Their values contrast with the code of freedom's price and the personal honor of Western heroism. Mottos such as "give me liberty or give me death" and "death before dishonor" do not resonate among the mujahideen. The hypothetic "death absolves dishonor" is more apropos in their world.

5

Modernization and Authenticity: Critique of Endeavors

In the preceding chapter we saw that the Islamic activists' approach to the plight of their society involves popular militarism. Left unsaid is that this response evolved consequent to the historic failure of Islamic states to match the West militarily. Modernization of the Islamic world effectively began with the efforts of the Ottoman elite to reverse the decline in military capability vis-à-vis the Europeans. In the early 1800s, regimes in Istanbul and Cairo earnestly imported Western advisors, weapons, training methods, and military manufacturing and engineering techniques. They also sent observers and delegations to countries in Europe to learn the ways of the West. However, decades of effort did not achieve the desired goal. Egypt's rapid militarization under Muhammad 'Ali Pasha was ended by the intervention of the European powers. The military reforms of the central Ottoman regime were not sufficient to avoid defeat in war with Russia in 1828–1829 and two wars with Muhammad 'Ali in 1831–1833 and 1838–1841. Nonetheless, there was considerable spin-off effect from the military modernization projects.

The government-directed attention to Europe's military manufacturing and engineering led to awareness of commercial manufacturing and civil engineering techniques. Similarly, the attention to Europe's military medical and veterinary services led to awareness of medical advances in general. Islamic society did not have such advanced technology and medical science. The regimes at Istanbul and Cairo were primarily concerned with military applications, and so they initiated systematic efforts to translate European works on military organization, training, armament, and support services. However, such translation activity inevitably spread to other subjects, which were already on the minds of those officials and designees who had been sent to Europe. They duly reported on factors of military strength, but they also brought back impressions of the West's social, economic, and political organization as well as its educational philosophy.

Such awareness posed dilemmas of modernization for most of the Ottoman ruling elite. Their goal was an increase in state power, not a radical transformation of society. The soldier–administrator class generally was not keen on popularizing philosophies that included quite alien and potentially subversive models of state–society and intra-societal relationships. The ulema class, with its near-monopoly on education, was not eager to change the curriculum of the *madrasas*. Indeed, the natural and physical "sciences" of the West correlated to branches of the ancillary subject of physics. These disciplines could not be on a par with the true sciences, such as Quran interpretation, theology, and jurisprudence. Yet, the more enlightened among the administrators, the ulema, and the non-Muslim intellectuals could accept that the strength of the West entailed much more than its war-making method and technology. Such individuals, in official and nonofficial capacities, took up the task of commending the adoption of certain Western institutions and practices as beneficial to societal reform and progress.

One of the earliest advocates of selective Westernization, particularly in the literary and educational arenas, was the Lebanese Christian Butrus al-Bustani (b. 1819). Being an employee and associate of the American consulate in Beirut, he was relatively safe from intimidation. On his own initiative, he wrote tracts and discourses on social and cultural issues; published translations, textbooks, a newspaper, and a journal; launched an encyclopedia project; and opened a secondary school to teach a modern curriculum. Another educator and admirer of the West was Bustani's older contemporary Rifa'a al-Tahtawi (b. 1801) of Egypt. Unlike Bustani, the Muslim Tahtawi made his career in governmental service. Moreover, he gained direct experience of European society when he served five years as the imam of an Egyptian educational mission in Paris. Tahtawi was an author, teacher, school administrator, member of commissions, and editor of an official newspaper and journal. His major contribution, however, was in the state's translation program. He himself translated some twenty French works on history, geography, and military science and directed the translation of numerous other books. His book on Egyptian society (*Manâhij al-Albâb*) endorsed a state-led approach to modernization, including educational and legal reform and promotion of patriotism and progress.

The endeavors of Bustani, Tahtawi, and their respective circles were paralleled by those of similar-minded intellectuals—the so-called "Young Ottomans"—in Istanbul. There, the effort of translating the literary forms and ideas of Western public edification was associated with the three publicists Ibrahim Şinasi (b. 1826), Ziya Paşa (b. 1825), and Namık Kemal

(b. 1840). Of the three, Namık Kemal became the most prominent. Like other advocates of reform, he spent some years in Europe, although his status was that of self-exile. He was a translator, a journal and newspaper editor, and the author of essays, articles, novels, plays, and poems that conveyed the merits of Western ideas and institutions. Namık Kemal's foremost contribution was promoting the ideas of fatherland (*vatan*) and freedom (*hürriyet*), albeit as values consistent with Islamic tradition. For him, fatherland was a new symbol to motivate society, and freedom was the outcome of constitutional controls on government. His ideas were considered too subversive, and so the regime banished him from the capital, in one way or another, during much of his later life.

As for reformist statesmen, two of the most renowned were Khayr al-Din (Pasha) al-Tunisi and Ahmet Vefik Paşa. Khayr al-Din (b. 1810) began his career in the military service of the Bey of Tunis, an Ottoman vassal. Like Tahtawi, he had the opportunity to spend years in Paris on official duty. On his return to Tunis, he became Minister of Marine and leader of a constitutionalist movement that sought to limit the prerogatives of the Bey and his court. A constitution for the beylik was in fact promulgated in 1860, but it was suspended in 1864 because of various problems. At that point, Khayr al-Din withdrew from official activity and wrote a treatise on government which pointed to Western practices as being factors of strength—representative and responsible government, free press, and enlightened education. He was consequently invited to Istanbul, where he initially enjoyed the Sultan's confidence and served as grand vizier for a year. However, his efforts to pursue reform there were negated by the same problems he had encountered in Tunis—financial chaos, conservative resistance, and foreign interference.

The Ottoman governmental reform movement eventually did achieve the promulgation of a constitution in 1876. Consequently, Ahmet Vefik Paşa became the first Chairman of the Chamber of Deputies. As an adolescent, Ahmet (b. 1823) had gone with his father to Paris where he attended the Lycée St. Louis. Upon his return to Istanbul, he collaborated with the chief architects of the early reform programs, the *Tanzimat*. He also served the Ottoman state as grand vizier twice—albeit briefly—and as ambassador at Paris and Tehran. In the arena of public edification, he compiled a Turkish dictionary, translated several French literary works, wrote plays, and promoted theater-going. Ahmet Vefik sought first and foremost to strengthen the state; he advocated a gradualist approach to social change. Thus, he may not have been distressed when the constitution was suspended in February 1878.

The endeavors of these five prominent "modernizers" were complemented by those of hundreds of others who are not mentioned here. Notoriety aside, the significant point is that their collective thoughts reflected key movements of the Western world of the early nineteenth century: (1) the Industrial Revolution and its associated epistemology (philosophy of knowledge) and philosophy of science, (2) constitutionalism, and (3) societal mobilization, whose ethos was passing from revolutionary to nationalist. What each of the modernizers took from these movements varied greatly depending on faith, career, and other personal circumstances. The majority within Ottoman society, though, were not so receptive to the ways of the West. Either they objected outright to borrowing alien ideas and practices or they saw greater advantage in reviving pristine Islamic virtues. Such disinclination was reinforced by a surge of European imperialism within the Ottoman dominion, which included the Russian exploitation of the Balkan uprisings in 1877, the Austrian occupation of Bosnia in 1878, the French occupation of Tunis in 1881, and the British occupation of Egypt in 1882.

Among those who advocated a uniquely Islamic approach to modernization, the first prominent ideologue was the enigmatic Jamal al-Din al-Afghani (b. 1838/39), whose origin and place of birth are obscure. Al-Afghani traveled widely throughout the Islamic world, studied at many centers of learning, and gained the confidence of the powerful, including the Shah of Persia and the Ottoman Sultan. His penchant for agitation in the cause of reform, however, often undid his welcome at their courts. He was insistent that Muslims unify in the face of Western imperialism and develop active virtue by discarding their aversion to philosophy. Concerning philosophy, al-Afghani was by no means an advocate of the materialist and naturalist approaches current in the West. These he discredited in his famous *Refutation of the Materialists*, whose line of argument is criticism of the Western-inspired, secularist thinking of Sayyid Ahmad Khan. Al-Afghani advocated, rather, the revival of (his ideal) of early Islamic philosophy, which tempered rationalism with respect for the importance of religion in human life. Such thinking suggests that suspicions of his Persian Shi'i origin may be correct because appreciation for philosophy had survived in Shi'ism.

Amid his wanderings, al-Afghani spent an eight-year span (1871–1879) in Egypt. There he acquired a circle of disciples that included the intellectual Muhammad 'Abduh and the later nationalist politician Sa'd Zaghlul. Jamal al-Din was seemingly more adept at speaking than writing his thoughts, but he inspired his students to write and publish. The association with 'Abduh (b. 1849) turned out to be particularly opportune. 'Abduh translated *The Refutation* into Arabic and joined his former teacher in exile in Paris, where they launched the periodical *al-'Urwa al-Wuthqâ* (the Firmest Bond) in 1884. That journal was their means of criticizing the Great Powers', and particularly Britain's, policy regarding the Muslim world, as well as of exhorting Muslims to reform themselves. Paris was also the scene of Jamal al-Din's famous controversy with the French scholar Renan over the compatibility of Islam and modernity. Al-Afghani took to further travels, Russia and Persia, to find the right champion for his causes, but to no avail. He ended life at Istanbul under the watchful eye of the regime. The movement that he started became known as "Islamic Modernism;" its hallmark is the use of reason to reinterpret the Qur'anic message.

As for Muhammad 'Abduh, he gave up the provocative tactics of al-Afghani and became the intellectual leader of the Islamic Modernist movement. From Paris, he moved to Beirut, where he taught at a Muslim school, discoursed with associates, and refined his ideas on theology, which were eventually published in his most influential book *Risâlat al-Tawhîd*. In 1888, 'Abduh was allowed to return to Egypt, but the government attempted to direct his energy away from education toward the judicial arena. He served as judge in high-level courts and, in 1899, became the *muftî* (head religious law authority) of Egypt and a member of the Legislative Council, which was actually a high-governmental advisory council. From those positions of influence, he brought about reforms in the administration of Islamic law and religious endowments. 'Abduh was also able to induce reforms in the administration and curriculum of al-Azhar, where he lectured and "lobbied" for reform of the ulema establishment. His successes there multiplied because al-Azhar was and continued to be the pre-eminent (Sunni) center of Islamic learning. Its graduates carried 'Abduh's ideas to the far corners of the Islamic world.

As with any deep thinking, 'Abduh's ideas were interpreted and developed differently by his many disciples. They inevitably met with criticism, especially from conservatives. 'Abduh's aim was to reconcile the inherent religiosity of his native society with the inherent secularism of inevitable modernization. The resolution of that dilemma could not be free of contestable points in its methodology. As Albert Hourani adeptly observed:

> It may be that 'Abduh's view of Islam was itself affected by his view of what the modern mind needs. He carried further a process we have already seen . . . that of identifying certain concepts of Islamic thought with the dominant ideas of modern Europe. In this line of thought, *maslaha* gradually turns into utility, *shura* into parliamentary democracy, *ijma'* into public opinion; Islam itself becomes identical with civilization and activity.[1]

The outcome might well be a distortion of original meaning or arbitrariness in the selection and correlation of concepts.

Controversy notwithstanding, 'Abduh's thought influenced several leading Muslim intellectuals of Egypt, including Qasim Amin, Lutfi al-Sayyid, and 'Ali Abd al-Raziq. It likewise influenced several leading Muslim intellectuals of Syria, including his also-famous disciple Rashid Rida. It was Rida's periodical *al-Manâr* that further publicized various themes of Islamic Modernism and particularly the concept of salafism, which did not then have the militant overtone that it has now. The salafism of Rida, following 'Abduh and al-Afghani, was the belief that the deeds of the first generation(s) of Muslims serve as models for active virtue in the present day. Rida, in his turn, influenced the thinking of Hasan al-Banna, founder of the Muslim Brotherhood, which promotes self-help, Islamic ethics, and criticism of inept government. Elsewhere in the Arab world, 'Abduh's ideas directly influenced the establishment of the Association of Algerian Reformist Ulema in 1931. It is also likely, but less explicitly so, that Muhammad 'Abduh influenced modernist intellectuals in India, where al-Afghani had challenged the views of Sayyid Ahmad Khan and his followers. Muslim India would be another home of Islamic modernist genius, as seen in the work of Muhammad Iqbal and, later, Fazlur Rahman.

Overall, the spread of reformist and modernist ideas was affected by new developments in the aftermath of World War I. The consequence of Ottoman defeat in that war was the continuation of European occupation of the North African littoral and new occupation of the League of Nation mandates in the Levant and Mesopotamia. The focus in the Arab lands turned toward nationalist assertion and agitation for independence. Turkey, which had preserved its independence, followed Atatürk's program of Westernization. Iran, not to be surpassed by an historic adversary, pursued a similar course. These various currents were either interrupted or reversed by the outbreak of World War II, as Allied Forces safeguarded Egypt and intervened in Iraq and Iran. The end of that conflict led to the bipolar antagonism between the Capitalist First World (Western Bloc) and the Communist Second World (Eastern Bloc) and the relegation of most Muslim countries to the Third World.

The Third World was a diverse collection, yet it supposedly manifested the common characteristics of (1) formerly foreign-occupied or foreign-protected territory and (2) economic and socio-political underdevelopment. In the aftermath and as an outcome of World War II, the colonial masters (or occupiers) accepted that it was opportune to grant independence and withdraw militarily. However, the Western Bloc could not break or avoid ties with strategically important lands. Thus, there evolved considerable interest in foreign assistance and "development science." The latter essentially encompassed the critique of conditions in traditional (that is, nonmodern, non-Westernized) societies and the creation of theories and programs to abet their economic, social, and political development. The adepts of "development" saw the overall objective as positive change or progress as defined by the experience of the West, particularly the Industrial Revolution. This new discipline emerged from several foundational studies—with perhaps the foremost being Talcott Parsons's *The Social System* (1951). In its earlier years, the study of development gave priority to the economic factor, with the dominant model being W. W. Rostow's famous treatise, *The Stages of Economic Growth* (1960). In time, theorists accepted that the economic factor was not all-determining, and more attention was given to social and political factors. Development theory passed through phases of critique (dependency theory) and counter-critique (dependent development) and more recently acknowledged the significance of cultural difference. The corollary was that the path to progress must have authenticity: that is, conformity with the native culture, not with an alien culture.

Late-twentieth-century development theory presupposes the existence of civil society, which is of dubious relevance to the Third World in general and to Islamic society in particular. It also takes for granted the existence of two enabling factors: an innovative–entrepreneurial class and a "professional" bureaucracy that works according to legal and ethical codes for the stewardship of public assets and services. In actuality, for the tribal/clan-oriented ethic of Islamic society, the concepts of civility (genuine tolerance for "the other") and public goods are meaningless. An asset cannot be possessed or controlled except by one clan or another, and the competition for it precludes social cohesion and abets feuding. The historic solution in the Islamic world has been authoritarian government—and this observation is empirical, not judgmental.

It took decades of criticism to dispel the conviction that the only way to development, or modernity, was the Western way. One of the more vehement critics in the mid-1990s assessed the "development discourse" as follows: "Development was—and continues to be for the most part—a top-down, ethnocentric, and technocratic approach that treats peoples and cultures as abstract concepts, statistical figures to be moved up and down in the charts of 'progress' . . . [and] a response to the problematization of poverty . . . not a natural process of knowledge."[2] Indeed, regarding Islamic society, the development "experts" ignored the decades of native intellectual and practical efforts to achieve modernization. More surprisingly, the governmental leaders within the Islamic world were receptive to their tutelage on development planning.

On the positive side, the development science community has started to realize that there are other paths to modernization. The East Asian boom, which was once attributed to the import of democracy and laissez faire economics, is now seen to be the outcome of "new authoritarianism" or "Confucian capitalism." Yes, there was, and remains, an element of authoritarianism in economic management; and yes, there was an element of reviving ancient virtue in the East Asian experience. The well-documented, post–World War II effort whereby the eventual boom countries systematically rewrote textbooks demonstrates the efficacy of native cultural influence.[3] That endeavor to "revitalize" Confucian teachings can be seen as a replay of the Renaissance effort to revitalize the

works of Classical Antiquity. The common denominator is the revitaliza-
tion of historically old but culturally coherent values. The argument for
authenticity within the development discourse was certainly a turn in
the right direction. Yet, by the time it emerged, both classic development
theory and the indigenous modernization movement were being
discredited by Islamic activists in the Islamic world. For them, the former
was a secularist insult to the Islamic way of life and another form of
Western imperialism; the latter was at best too passive and at worst too
tainted.

Indeed, both the reformist and Islamic Modernist "schools" that
emerged in the Islamic world had recognized that the fundamental
problem with their society was ethics. However, neither solved the
challenge of forging a new ethical code that was both authentic and
progressive. The reformists' efforts to "translate" Western values and
forms of expression into native ones did little to change the indigenous
ethics per se. The Modernists' thinking evolved largely as controversy
over how and what to save of the religious heritage. Their efforts to
reform the educational establishment became a debate over the right
balance between the traditional—mainly religious—disciplines and the
modern sciences in school and college curricula. The real necessity was to
forge a new ethic to inspire active endeavors to improve society.

Again, Ibn Khaldun's historiography serves, albeit in a somewhat
different sense, to elucidate the situation. Several aspects of the *Prolegomena* (*al-Muqaddima*) are particularly relevant to the modernization
discourse within Islamic society. One is Ibn Khaldun's focus on humanity
as it really exists in physical and social environments. Another is his
assessment of the natural causes of the rise and demise of regimes. Yet a
third is his assertion that prophethood is not necessary for human
existence. So it transpired that Tahtawi encouraged the publication of the
whole *Kitâb al-'Ibar*, as one of the Arabic classics, at the government press
at Bulâq. At about the same time, the Ottoman statesman Cevdet Paşa
produced a complete Turkish translation of *al-Muqaddima*. Despite such
interest, Ibn Khaldun's thesis was not welcome with conservatives.
Muhammad 'Abduh proposed the inclusion of *al-Muqaddima* in the
curriculum of al-Azhar. The Shaykh (Rector) of al-Azhar responded that
"it would be against the tradition of teaching" at that institution.[4] The
more significant point, however, is that the reformists missed the negative
implications of Ibn Khaldun's theory of *'aṣabîya* as it relates to social cohesion and public interest.

In the end, there was no effective solution from the Western- or Islamic-
inspired reformist movements or from the development management
arena. Like the earlier military modernization and industrialization
programs, the development plans and projects generally made a few
natives wealthy but increased foreign debt, set up infrastructure and

machinery that was not efficiently operated or maintained, and left the populace dispirited. The way was open for the activist fundamentalists to "seize the moment." The Islamic Modernists had already made significant strides by encouraging reinterpretation of the Qur'anic message. However, their method was too dependent on rationalism, which had been rejected over and over in the course of Islamic history. In any case, the Modernists' "rereading" of the Qur'an deduced that its main theme was the implementation of social justice, or equity. They averred that this condition was what God intended for human existence.

The Islamist intellectuals who tended away from modernism toward fundamentalism were keen to develop the social justice theme. The ethics were imbedded in Qur'anic revelation, and the role models were known from Islamic hero lore. Their task was a matter of inducing the populace to awaken from its customary passivity and emulate the active virtue of the early Muslims. The pressing need was action, not rationalization. Some of the ideologues of Islamic activism, such as Maududi, took more moderate, political approaches to the task. However, popular self-help activism too often seemed to founder at the barriers of autocracy, class privilege, foreign interest, or governmental corruption. The inevitable reaction was resort to militancy, with its concomitant violence, as noted previously. Violence has yet to achieve the goals of the Islamist activists or to convince the moderate majority of Muslims. It brought down the Shah of Iran, but the country's socioeconomic problems persist. The apologists for Islamic activism have argued, and rightly so, that effective reform will take time. But what constitutes effective reform? The activists' approach to economic management, for example, cannot succeed in the present circumstances. They insist on reallocation of wealth. However, with many countries, the size of the economy compares negatively with the size of the population. Thus, reallocation of wealth can be nothing more than choosing which group or class to impoverish.

Discounting the lessons on jihad and martyrdom, the educational initiatives of the Islamic Republic of Iran offer some insights on the issue of effective reform. These concern deliberate instructional efforts to promote the values of unity, consultation, responsibility, and cooperation and to inculcate the virtues of *ithâr* (preference for the other) and *jehâd-e sazandeg* (effort to build).[5] These objectives clearly contribute to a progressive kind of ethics. However, they should be removed from the sponsorship of schools, which are likely distracted by their own priorities and interests. To afford the necessary reinforcement, developmental activities should be commissioned to new institutions. Such institutions would function like youth clubs of the West, but they must have native precedents to be seen as authentic, that is, culturally consistent. This is a daunting, yet feasible, endeavor. If ethics are to be reformed, the reform must take a certain direction. The way is shown through assessment of the critical problems, which, in light of the foregoing study, seem to be lack of civic consciousness, industriousness, and inventiveness. Thus, ethical reform should attempt to modify kin preference behavior, accord value to earnest work as a means to improve living conditions, and overcome the negativity of *bid'a* (innovation).

The problem with kin preference behavior, as an overly dominant tendency, may not be evident or even believable to most people in the West. It is tied, especially in Arab culture, to the dignity/shame (or honor/dishonor) complex—the imperative of gaining the former and avoiding the latter. Thus, judges in competitive undertakings might deny a contract, job, promotion, or trophy to the "objectively best" contender simply because he belongs to the "wrong clan." Conversely, a student would cheat on an exam and *not* feel shame when caught because his motive is to gain honor for his clan by attaining the highest score. The same can be said for "twisting the truth" to avoid disgracing one's own clan or to deflect dishonor onto another. Such behavior ostensibly discourages both cultivation of talent and objective (or fair) thinking about merit. As it is, talent is sought mainly to benefit special groups rather than all of society. Were it the latter case, society might place higher value on accomplishment. The drawbacks keep compounding, and that is hardly conducive to the building of a strong society and state. The objective, then, is to modify the attitudes that no one truly "counts" except kinsmen and clients and that one cannot do much about anything—the proverbial *"mâ 'alaysh"* reaction.

Fraternal organizations, or brotherhoods, dedicated to inculcating virtues existed in medieval times in the eastern lands of Islam. The origin, varieties, and interconnection of these brotherhoods have yet to be fully studied and clarified. Nonetheless, the generic term for them was Arabic *futûwa*, which connotes the virtues of young men—vigor, valor, nobleness, and chivalry. The *futûwa* fraternities were found among aristocracy, urban tradesmen, Sufi orders, and town militias. In modern times, the name has been applied to the youth organizations of political parties in some Arab countries. Therefore, current usage would have to be modified to dissociate the term from party organization. In any event, the precedent is authentic and serves well as a model for the present.

The grand task would be establishing these organizations by approximate age group to progress from basic learning objectives to more sophisticated ones. Three indispensable precepts are (1) teaching progressive concepts and values, (2) using projects to reinforce those values, and (3) assigning members of different clans and sects, as feasible, to each "club" and to each of its project groups. A committee of reform-oriented native educators and intellectuals should decide on the concepts and associated values. Some suggestions follow:

- Interdependence   cooperation, mutual responsibility, and (above all) trust
- Well-being   accomplishment and industriousness
- Community   contribution and preference for the other
- Objectivity   honesty, fairness, and respect for standards
- Value of job output   self-responsibility and conscientiousness
- Mutual benefit   general (public) welfare, inclusive "we"

The projects—the practical reinforcement—might involve handicrafts or simple manufacturing at lower levels, multi-component assembly at mid-level, and service system or network design at higher levels. Enabling learning objectives should include self-evaluation, product evaluation, comparison of like products, product enhancement, and so forth. One significant hurdle is that such clubs would have to be directed, at least initially, by well-qualified foreigners or Westernized natives.

Concurrent with the establishment of these youth clubs, the state educational ministries should review textbook content and curriculum guides. The discussion of the preceding chapter indicates the nature of the hero lore that exists in schoolbooks throughout the Islamic world. That survey does not represent the total picture, but it does reveal that there is too much correlation between militant jihad and active virtue. Revision committees could focus on those Companions of the Prophet, both males and females, who made nonmilitary contributions to the *umma*, showing diligence in tending the communal camel herd, showing exceptional virtue in judging fairly, and so forth. Beyond the Companions, the ghazis and leaders of jihads might be recast as men of just aims or humane dispositions, and, likewise, some of the modern day "nationalists." Perhaps a greater task than the effort of revision and republication would be the effort to introduce the revised texts into privately financed and administered schools.

Lastly, the problem of inventiveness might well be remedied through the revival of a second historic institution. This has variant names—*dâr al-ḥikma* (house of wisdom) in western lands of Islam and *dâr al-'ilm* (house of science) in the east. These were palace rooms, libraries, or residences where leading intellectuals met to discuss their own—and outsiders'—ideas and writings. They were more common among the Shi'a, although some were founded by Sunnis, and many had mixed affiliation. The institution disappeared from Islamic society as the Sunni Seljuk Turks consolidated their control of eastern Islam and other Sunni regimes displaced the Ismailis in the west. Some of the functions of the *dâr al-ḥikma/dâr al-'ilm* were taken up, in a way, at the madrasas. However, the madrasas, at present, are probably not the right hosts for new thought centers or "think tanks." These should be independently established. They should be organized and commissioned to undertake one or all of the following broad tasks, which generally equate to managed development. The first task would involve economics, specifically finding a way to justify capital formation given the indigenous aversion to "profit on investment."

The issue of capital formation is particularly troublesome because of the Qur'anic injunctions against usury, making profit (*ribḥ*) on loans. Dilemmas might be resolved by explaining the difference between the Prophet's time and the current time with respect to economic matters. However, such an approach founders on the strongly held belief that the Qur'anic revelation is not only eternal but also perfectly valid for all circumstances. In that sense, history does not matter; however, it should matter. The scripture clearly addresses the circumstances that existed in Muhammad's time, wherein some people treated others unfairly, despite economic sufficiency. There is no mention of starvation or lack of necessities. The thrust of the Qur'anic revelation is the remedying of inequities, as the Islamic activists and modernists both would agree. The overall remedy is the reallocation of wealth. Specific remedies are injunctions concerning inheritance, mandatory contribution to the poor, prohibition of profiteering, and division of war booty.

The sufficiency of wealth is taken for granted. But how can this be, given historical notions about pre-Islamic Arabia? The fact is that such notions, many of them generated in the West, are not historical at all, but romantic. The western Arabia of Muhammad's day was not an impoverished, backward land. It was part of a region-wide commercial network that emerged from the Sassanid Persian conquest first of Yemen and then of northern Mesopotamia, Syria-Palestine, and Egypt. It was the Byzantine effort, following military victory over the Persians, to re-occupy the Syrian frontier areas that led to confrontation with the Muslims. The Muslim Arabs not only negated the Byzantine effort but also reconstructed the Sassanid commercial empire, albeit on their own terms. They even went on to enlarge it through a dynamic of territorial conquest and border raid activity. This clarification of history may seem digressive, but it is extremely meaningful. Contemporary governments cannot resolve economic matters through reallocation of wealth when the amount of wealth available is not sufficient for all of society. The economic "pie" must be enlarged for everyone to get a piece. Unless this challenge is resolved, the growing, dispossessed youth population within the Islamic world has little choice but to follow the propaganda of the jihadists.

The second task for the thought centers would be to find new roles for government. Its historic functions as regard economic management and internal security are of questionable relevance. The functions of wealth acquisition (from internal and external sources) and wealth redistribution are of little consequence when the sources of wealth are insufficient for a growing populace. Moreover, gradual success of the above-mentioned *futûwa* project would eventually diminish the need for government to constrain factionalism—that is, keep clan rivalries and power-plays in check. The third task for the thought centers would be to complement other projects for reforming ethics and education. The centers could serve as commissions to review the progress of the *futûwa* or curriculum-revision projects. They could also sponsor the writing of a new kind of morals literature for children and students. Another worthwhile related enterprise would be sponsorship of the translation and publication of applicable works on applied science or the publication of a heritage series. The latter would entail the editing and publishing of Arabic works that influenced the rise of modern science in the West, for example, the books on alchemy that contributed to the development of chemistry and those on optics that led to an understanding of vision.

Regarding the "make-up" of the thought centers, they should reclaim the old name *dâr al-ḥikma* yet provide modern efficiencies for communications, research, publishing, collaboration, and so forth. Apart from a small administrative and house-keeping staff, the incumbents should be appointed for limited terms on a basis of merit. The creation of sinecures for "favorites" of the ruling establishment could be counterproductive. Conversely, the inclusion of minority sect members and foreign guest scholars might be advantageous.

Perhaps the Muslim intellectual elite can revive the spirit of inquiry and creativity that infused Islamic civilization in the distant past, and perhaps the people of the Islamic world can learn to temper their inherent distrust of nonrelatives or nonclients. They might also come to equate the concepts of *citizen* and *contributor* (to the general welfare of society). With those developments, they might learn productive uses of freedom—then would be the time for them to have freedom. Of course, foreign assistance money would be required for these projects, but the cost should be far less than the billions now spent on the war against terrorism and its spin-off conflicts. The more critical need, apart from time, would be willingness of indigenous regimes to (1) tolerate and support such projects as a modern *futûwa* and a modern *dâr al-ḥikma* and (2) heed and implement vetted ideas of the *dâr al-ḥikma* type institution.

In conclusion, the intellectual dynamics of contemporary Islamic society may be "graphed" in terms of an ends and means comparison of four currents of thought.

- Westernization   assimilation of secular ways of thinking and acting by disregarding the traditional religious ethos
- Reformism   assimilation of secular ways of thinking and acting by accommodating the traditional religious ethos

- Islamic Modernism   renewal of the religious ethos by using nontraditional ways of thinking
- Islamic Activism   renewal of the religious ethos by reviving pristine religious values

None of these movements has resolved the crisis of Islamic society—the dilemma of modernization. Perhaps the reason for this is that none of them has seriously considered the importance of humanistic ethics in the quest for modernity.

Appendix

The Emergence of Citizenship in Islamdom

Nawaf A. Salam

A man can be proud of his own deeds, not of his father's reputation
—Arab Poet

Tout homme est utile à l'humanité par cela seul qu'il existe
—J.J. Rousseau

The purpose of this article is to provide a framework for the understanding of the many dilemmas that have faced the emergence of the notion of citizenship in Islam.

It is divided into four parts. The first briefly outlines the evolution of the concept of citizenship leading to what has come to be widely recognized as forming its main features and components in the modern world. The second tries to identify in classical Islam the elements upon which the development of the idea of citizenship could draw. The third part of the article focuses on the changes in modern Ottoman times which made it possible for the concept of citizenship, in its modern sense, to take root. The final part is a conclusion which will attempt to shed some light on the tensions affecting the quest for citizenship in the Islamic world.

THE EVOLUTION OF CITIZENSHIP AND ITS FEATURES

The concept of citizenship is at least as old as the Greek *polis*. For Aristotle, "what effectively distinguishes the citizen proper from all others is his participation in giving judgment and in holding office."[1] He further clarifies this definition in relation to that of the state: "as soon as a man

---

[1] Aristotle, *The Politics*, translated by T. A. Sinclair, revised and re-presented by Trevor J. Saunders, London, 1981, p. 169.

becomes entitled to participate in office, deliberative or judicial, we deem him to be a citizen of that state; and a number of such persons large enough to secure a self-sufficient life we may, by and large, call a state."[2] But Aristotle also acknowledges that his definition does not apply to all times and places. "We see the various constitutions differing from each other in kind, some being prior to others. . . . A citizen, therefore, will necessarily vary according to the constitution in each case."[3]

In fact, in both ancient Greece and Rome, citizenship was a privilege of the few. In the "democracy" of the Greek city-states, women, slaves, and "resident foreigners"[4] were excluded from the status of citizenship.[5] In Rome, citizenship was the basic criterion which served to distinguish between the rights—both civil and political—of the Roman citizens (*civis*) and those of the populations of the conquered territories to whom citizenship was, only later, partially and gradually extended.[6]

In contrast to the modern meaning of citizenship,[7] the ancient concept of citizenship seems very exclusive and its attributes limited. The former has become inseparable from the idea of universal suffrage. The holding of citizens' rights as synonymous to "Human Rights" is also a developing trend. The characteristic features and historical development of citizenship in its modern meaning have been studied by a number of authors. Four of these author's leading works will be mentioned in order to illustrate the scope the notion of modern citizenship came to cover as well as the type of new questions being thus raised.

Marshall in a classic article, based on his study of the English experience, distinguished three components of citizenship and suggested that they were institutionalised according to the following sequence: First, the civil (referring to individual liberties and the rule of law); next, the political (associated with the democratic franchise and participation); and last, the social (concerned with the problems of "welfare").[8] Interested in the role of "social movements" in the development of citizenship, Turner identified four successive "waves"[9] associated with the role played by different factors in the definition of citizenship:

---

[2] *Idem*, p.171.
[3] *Idem*, p. 170.
[4] *Idem*, p. 169.
[5] See generally, Finley, Moses I., *Democracy Ancient and Modern*, revised edition, New Brunswick, 1985: *Idem, Economy and Society in Ancient Greece*, New York, 1982.
[6] See generally, Grant, Michael, *History of Rome*, New York, 1978; *Idem, The World of Rome*, New York, 1960 (chs. 3 and 4) and Nicolet, Claudine, *Le métier de citoyen dans la Rome Républicaine*, seconde édition revue et corrigée, Paris, 1976 (chs. 1 and 7).
[7] Which could be dated to the two landmark texts: the American *Declaration of Independence* (1776) and the French *Declaration des Droits de l'Homme et du Citoyen* (1789).
[8] See Marshall, T. H., *Class, Citizenship and Social Development*, Garden City, 1965, pp. 71–134.
[9] See Turner, Bryan S., *Citizenship and Capitalism*, London, 1986, pp 85–105.

1. Property;
2. Sex;
3. Kinship ties and age; and
4. Current environmental problems.[10]

Shifting the focus to the individual, Ullman considers the passage from medieval to modern times to correspond to the transition from subjects to "full fledged citizens."[11] As for Leca, the crisis of modern citizenship seems to lie in the "logical dilemma" and yet, "sociological necessity" of the combination of two contradictory principles in our societies: that of the "private" and that of the "participatory" individual.[12]

Centuries of social and political change separate, indeed, the ancient city-state idea of citizenship from that of modern times. To say the least, these centuries have witnessed revolutionary developments such as the extension of citizenship membership to formerly excluded categories, the reformulation of the meaning of "participation," the foundation of citizens' rights on new ethical bases and the redefinition of their reach, leading to the emergence of new citizenship aspirations. Yet, the very idea of citizenship, throughout its evolution, has always evoked the following: the existence of a state, the recognition of the individual, and relationship between the two of them based on membership. This membership gave the individuals entitlement to certain rights (most importantly that of participation in political decisions) and required the discharge of certain duties.

That citizenship is bound to the existence of a state is best shown by the fact that a stateless person is not a citizen.[13] Today, the international community recognises the former's "Human Rights," but only a state can bestow on him citizenship. And while the legal bond of "nationality" conveys the notion of belonging to a state,[14] citizenship adds to that a sense of membership in a political community invested with sovereignty.

"Constitutive of the state, the individual citizen is also constituted by it. For only equality before the universal law makes possible his liberation, in

---

[10] "The fourth wave of expanding citizenship rights, writes Turner, is brought about by social movements which in fact have the consequence of ascribing rights to nature and the environment. Social movements to protect nature from human exploitation are attributing rights to animal and organic phenomena in the same way that said movements in the nineteenth century ascribed rights to women and the working class." *Idem*, p. 98.

[11] See Ullman, Walter, *The Individual and Society in the Middle Ages*, Baltimore, 1966, pp. 101–151.

[12] Leca, Jean "Individualisme et citoyenneté" in Birnbaum, Pierre and Leca, Jean, sous la direction de, *Sur l'individualisme*, Paris, 1986, p. 207.

[13] See Arendt, Hannah, "Imperialism" in *The Burden of Our Time*, London, 1951, pp. 121–238 quoted in Balibar, Etienne: "Propositions on Citizenship" in *Ethics*, 98, July 1988, p. 726.

[14] On the subject and related distinctions, see generally, Kossler, Maximillian, "Subject, citizen, national and permanent allegiance" in *Yale Law Journal*, Vol. 56, 1946, pp. 58–76.

the abstract, from the solidarity networks and domination based on par-
ticularisms,"[15] writes Leca. In fact, one of the features of modern citizenship
is that it developed through the tension between the two opposing principles of communality and individuality. Citizenship is a status conferred on
persons admitted, *as individuals*, to legal membership in a political community; and "all who possess this status, as Marshall observes, are equal
with respect to the rights and duties with which the status is endowed."[16]
Accordingly, modern citizenship has aimed to eliminate all forms of hered-
itary or group privilege and requires that persons, as individual citizens,
be equal before the law. Yet, in its core values, citizenship is not opposed
to social and economic inequalities as such but, in the words of Marshall,
"to illegitimate inequality, to inequality which cannot be justified on a
basis of equal citizenship rights."[17]

Citizenship rights derive then from the citizen's status and through
them the latter is transformed into an "accomplished and achieved reality."[18]
Central among those rights is the "participatory" right, i.e., the citizen's
right to participate in the exercise of political power. It includes both the
right to vote and the right to hold office which, in their modern meanings,
became synonymous to universal suffrage and equality of opportunity,
respectively. Their denial to certain categories may only rest on "legitimate"
grounds; for example, legal incapacity due to age.

Another characteristic of modern citizenship is the increasing redefinition of citizens' duties in terms of "responsibility towards the welfare of
the community."[19] They generally include the payment of taxes, military
service and, in some societies, education.[20]

THE ELEMENTS IN CLASSICAL ISLAM UPON WHICH
CITIZENSHIP COULD DRAW

It has been previously stated that the recognition of the individual is
one of the fundamental components of citizenship. Hence, identifying
the elements of individualism in classical Islam seems a warranted
starting point for this part of our enquiry, especially since it is the
encounter of those elements in the nineteenth century with the modern

---

[15] Leca, Jean, *op. cit.*, p. 186.

[16] Marshall, *op. cit.*, p. 92.

[17] *Idem*, p. 85.

[18] F. Barbalet, J. M., *Citizenship, Rights, Struggle and Class Inequalities*, Minneapolis, 1988,
pp. 15–16.

[19] Marshall, T. H., *op. cit.*, p. 123.

[20] For a discussion of the redefinition of citizenship duties - in general, see Janowitz, Morris,
"Observations on the Sociology of Citizenship: Obligations and Rights" in *Social Forces*,
Vol. 59, Sept. 1980, pp. 1–26.

ideas coming from Europe that laid the groundwork for the emergence of the modern idea of citizenship in Islamdom. This will be followed by a discussion of the questions of equality and political participation in Islam, successively.

The Elements of Individualism

When individualism is invoked, Michel Foucault is right to insist that three things ought to be distinguished:

> 1) The individualistic attitude, characterized by the absolute value attributed to the individual in his singularity and by the degree of independence conceded to him *vis-à-vis* the group to which he belongs and institutions to which he is answerable; 2) the positive valuation of private life, that is, the importance granted to family relationships, to the forms of domestic activity, and to the domain of patrimonial interests; 3) the intensity of the relations to self, that is, of the forms in which one is called upon to take oneself as an object of knowledge and a field of action, so as to transform, correct, and purify oneself and find salvation.[21]

Although it is the first of these three attitudes which is most pertinent to the development of citizenship, we should not totally disregard the other two for they are often interconnected and yet, bear in mind that such links "are neither constant nor necessary."[22]

The main trend in "Orientalism" has always stressed the "holistic"[23] nature of Islamic societies, past and present; that is their valorisation of the social whole and neglect or subordination to that end of the human individual. Very representative of that school of thought, with respect to classical Islam is Franz Rosenthal,[24] who writes:

> Islam *in principle* stresses the unique worth of the individual, provided that *all* his actions are directed toward the maintenance of the social structure of which his is part. . . . As Islam developed, religious ethics in its *totality* was conceived

---

[21] Foucault, Michel, *Le Souci de Soi*, Paris, 1976, pp. 56–57. English translation by Robert Hurley, *The Care of the Self*, New York, 1986, p. 42.

[22] *Idem*, p. 57.

[23] On "Holism," as opposed to "individualism," see generally, Dumont, Louis, *Homo hierarchicus, essai sur le système des castes*, Paris, 1966, and *idem*, *Essais sur l'individualisme. Une perspective anthropologique sur l'idéologie moderne*, Paris, 1983.

[24] See also, Badie, Bertrand, *Les deux Etats. Pouvoir et sociéte en Occident et en terre d'Islam*, Paris, 1986; Coulson, N. J., "The State and Individual in Islamic Law" in *International and Comparative Law Quarterly*, Vol. 6, Jan. 1957, pp. 49–60; Lambton, Ann K. S., *State and Government in Medieval Islam; An Introduction to the Study of Islamic Political Theory: The Jurists*, Oxford, 1981; and Sandler, R., "The Changing Concept of the Individual" in Savory, R. N. (ed.), *Introduction to Islamic Civilization*, Cambridge, 1976, pp. 137–145.

as aiming at service to society. . . . It was the *Umma*, or rather the *Jama'a*, the community that was the intended beneficiary of *whatever* an individual was supposed to do or not to do. Individual salvation depended *in the first place* on acting in concert with the rest of society and in acting for the good of one's fellow men.[25]

There can be no doubt that Islamic tradition attached a high value not only to the Umma[26] (the community of the believers), as such, but to the ideal of its unity as well. To the transcendent aspiration for unity corresponded not only an urge for solidarity but a need for conformity as well. This did not lead, however, as we shall attempt to show, to the total subordination of the individual's autonomy. Rather, it points to a constant tension in Islamic civilisation between the individual and the community. This is a sister tension to the greater one, indeed, which profoundly marked Islamic history: that between the universal message of Islam and the tribal organisation of society.[27]

As a preliminary remark, it should be noted that Islam inherited from Arab antiquity, the *Jahiliyya*, a considerable interest in personality[28] and character. This was demonstrated by S. D. Goitein's research[29] which was prompted by the following three observations that had caught his

---

[25] Rosenthal, Franz, " 'I am You': Individual Piety and Society in Islam" in Banani, Amin and Vryonis, Speros Jr. (eds.), *Individualism and Conformity in Classical Islam*, Wiesbaden, 1977, p. 53 (emphasis added). See also, *idem*, *The Muslim Concept of Freedom prior to the Nineteenth Century*, Leiden, 1960. For a different view on the question of freedom in classical Islam and a critique of the approach adopted in the latter work, see al-Arawi, Abdullah, *Mafhum al-Hurriya*, Casablanca, 1981.

[26] Generally see Massignon, Louis, "L'Umma et ses synonymes" in *Revue des Etudes Islamiques*, 1946, pp. 151–7; Van Nieuwenhuijze, C. A. O., "The Ummah, An Analytic Approach, in *Studia Islamica*, Vol. X, 1959, pp. 5–22; and Al-Sayyid, Radwan, *Al-ummah wa'l-jama'at wa'l-sultat*, Beirut, 1984, pp. 17–87.

[27] The pervasive role of blood and kinship ties in Islamic history is best shown in Ibn Khaldun, *The Muqaddimah: an Introduction to History*, translated by Franz Rosenthal, 3 Vols., Princeton, 2nd edn., 1967. For modern perspectives on the subject, see generally, Khoury, Philip S. and Kostiner, Joseph (eds.), *Tribes and State Formation in the Middle East*, Berkeley, 1990.

[28] On the development of the notion of "persons" in Arab antiquity and Islam, we still lack an in depth work comparable to Mauss, Marcel, "Une categorie de L'esprit humain: La notion de personne, celle de 'moi,'" originally published in *Journal of the Royal Anthropological Institute*, Vol. LXVIII, 1938, and later in his collected essays, *Sociologie et anthropologie*, Paris, 1950, pp. 331–62. Pertinent remarks on the subject can, however, be found in Massignon, Louis, "Le respect de la personne humaine en Islam et la priorite du droit d'asile sur le devoir de juste guerre" in *Revue International de la Croix Rouge*, Juin 1952, p. 445 and f; and in Fakhry, Majid, "Iktishaf al-insan al-arabi," originally published in *Al-kadaya al-mu'asira*, Vol. 1, 1963, pp. 14–23, and later in his collected essays, *Dirasat fi al-fikr al-arabi*, Beirut, 1977, pp. 289–303.

[29] Goitein, S. D., "Individualism and conformity in Classical Islam" in Banani, Amin and Vryonis, Speros Jr., *op. cit.*, pp. 3–17.

attention: first, the "endless number of individuals whose personality is clearly brought out"[30] in the Books of Arabic prose and poetry;[31] "the profuse richness of the Arabic language in words for character and character traits[32] proving that the ancient Arabs had a keen eye . . . for the personality of an individual with whom they had dealings,"[33] third, "the fantastic abundance of personal names, each with its own meaning . . . among the 65,000 or so persons listing in the *Jamhara*, several thousands . . . bear unique names, *Hapax Legomena*, not shared with others."[34]

In Islam, although the Koran emphasises the contradictions of man, describing him on the one hand as "weak,"[35] "foolish,"[36] "hasty,"[37] "unjust,"[38] "forgetful,"[39] and on the other as endowed with intelligence, "favoured," and "far above most of our creation,"[40] it remains that man is above all dignified for God "breathes into him of his spirit"[41] and establishes him as His "viceroy"[42] (*Khalifah*) on earth.

Man in the Koran is also made aware of his individual responsibility for his deeds before God:

> On that Day when all men come forward, cut off from one another, to be shown their [past] deeds, and so, he who shall have done an atom's weight of good, shall behold it, and he who shall have done an atom's weight of evil, shall behold it.[43]

And

> That no bearer of burdens shall be made to bear another's burden, and that nought shall be accounted unto man but what he is striving for.[44]

---

[30] *Idem*, p. 3.
[31] Mostly referred to here is Al Baladhuri, *Ansab al-Ashraf, edited by S. D. Goitien, Jerusalem, 1936*.
[32] Mostly referred to here is Ibn Sida al Mursi, *Al-Mukhassas fi'l-lugha*, Cairo: Bulaq, 1898–1903.
[33] Goitein, S. D., *op. cit.*, pp. 5–6.
[34] *Idem;* The *Jamhara* here cited is Hisham Ibn Muhammad al-Kalbi, *Jamharat Ansab al-Arab*, edited by Werner Caskel, Leiden, 1966; Generally for the continuation under Islam of the pre-Islamic interest in personal biographies and personality characteristics and its development through *'ilm al-rijal* (Study of men) into a major branch of Islamic literature, see *idem*, pp. 15–16.
[35] Koran (4, 28).
[36] *Idem* (33, 72).
[37] *Idem* (18, 11).
[38] *Idem* (14, 34).
[39] *Idem* (10, 12).
[40] *Idem* (17, 70).
[41] *Idem* (32, 9).
[42] *Idem* (2, 30).
[43] *Idem* (49, 6–8).
[44] *Idem* (53, 38 & 39).

Moreover, since there is no church or priesthood in Islam,[45] the believer's relationship with God should remain unmediated, thereby, confirming the former's individuality in his aloneness before the Creator.

As noted earlier, the main trend in "Orientalist" studies considers that these principles stressing the unique worth and individuality of human beings were defeated by a practice that increasingly subjected the individual's freedom and autonomy to the welfare of the community and the interests of the state. However, reviewing the main features of the individual's situation in the development of Islamic law—from its Koranic "principles" into an elaborate legal system—will provide us with a striking example that shows how such an extreme position fails to account for a "practice" rather dominated by the tension—referred to earlier—between the individual and the communal.

In support of his conclusion that "a system of guaranteed individual liberties" is simply "denied by the fundamental doctrines of the *Shari'a* itself,"[46] Coulson cites the ruler's discretionary powers with regard to methods of procedure (particularly in criminal cases)[47] and to the determination of offence and sanction,[48] the absence in the *Shari'a* of a real system of organised appeal,[49] and the fact that it lacks "such system as 'Droit administratif' to provide a real remedy against the abuse of individual rights by government bodies."[50] But such an approach to the subject from "too narrow an angle that of penal law,"[51] cannot appreciate as Schacht demonstrates, how "the *solutions* provided by Islamic law go decisively and consistently in favor of the rights of the individual, of the sanctity of contracts and of private property, and [how] they put severe limits to the action of the state in these matters."[52]

In fact, although Islamic law does not recognise the complete liberty of contracts, *pacta sunt servanda* remains one of its basic rules and finds its equivalent in the following two maxims: *al-muslimun ala shurutihum* (the Muslims are bound by their stipulations) and *al-shart amlak* (the stipulation prevails).[53] The respect for private property is not only a rule between

---

[45] "La rahbaniyya fi-l Islam" (No monkery in Islam) says a Prophet's *Hadith* as reported in Ahmad Ibn Hanbal, *Al-Musnad*, Vol. VI, Cairo, 1930, p. 226.
[46] Coulson, N. J., *op. cit.*, p. 60.
[47] *Idem*, p. 52.
[48] *Idem*, p. 53.
[49] *Idem*, p. 58.
[50] *Idem*.
[51] Schacht, Joseph, "Islamic law in Contemporary states" in *The American Journal of Comparative Law*, 19, p. 138, note 12.
[52] *Idem* (emphasis added).
[53] See *Idem*, p. 139, also Al Sanhuri, Abd al Razzaq, *Masadir al-Hagg fi al-Fiqh al-Islami*, Vols. 1 and 3, Cairo, 1954.

private persons but applies as well in their relationship with the state.[54] Additionally, the way in which both succession[55] and the establishment of *wakf*[56] (Mortmain) "technically function" is also "strictly individualist."[57]

In principle, the main purpose of the Islamic state is to uphold the *Shari'a* and the goal of government is to enable the individual believer to follow the good Muslim life of "enjoining the good and forbidding the evil" (*al-amr bi'l-ma'ruf wa'l-nahi an al-munkar*).[58] Yet, the relationship of the believer to the state was mainly defined in terms of an obligation of obedience and submission. It was justified by the fact that the very existence and maintenance of the state are necessary for the individual's fulfillment of his religious duty. But an important exception to the obligation was, again in principle, found in the maxim of "no obedience in sin" based on the Prophet's *Hadith*: "To hear and obey is binding, so long as one is not commanded to disobey (God); when one is commanded to disobey (God), he shall not hear or obey."[59] However, both in "practice" and in the development of mainstream Islamic political thought, priority was given to the cohesion of the community and to the internal peace of the state over the individual's possible recourse to the exception of the above-mentioned maxim. The "authoritarian view"[60] which triumphed in classical Islam went as far as holding that when the unity of the *Umma* was in danger and when need be to avoid chaos, submission ought to be given to the ruler, even if an evil doer or tyrannical. Al'Ash'ari, the representative *par excellence* of the "authoritarian view," was for example to denounce "the error of those who hold it right to rise against the Imams whensoever there may be apparent in them a falling away from right."[61]

It appears then that while the primacy accorded to the community gradually divested the individual of the most fundamental "civic" right he was entitled to—that of "opposition" to evil doing—this did not lead to his total subordination to communal interest. He was still recognised,

---

[54] See *Idem*, p. 140, in particular the paragraph quoted for *Kitab al-Kharaj* to where Abu Yusuf says: "It is neither lawful for the Imam, nor has he the power to give as a concession to anyone that which belongs to a Muslim or to a protected person, or to deprive them from anything which they possess, except he has a legal claim against them; in this case, he may exact from them that to which he has the right."

[55] See *Idem*, p. 138.

[56] See *idem*, p. 139.

[57] *Idem*.

[58] See generally, Gardet, Louis, *La Cité Musulmane. Vie sociale et politique*, Paris, 1976; and Gibb, H. A. R., "Constitutional organization" in Khadduri, Majid and Liebesny, Herbert J. (eds.), *Law in the Middle East*, Vol. I, Washington, D.C., 1955, pp. 3–27. For a different perspective on the subject see Al-Arawi, Abdallah, *Mafhum al-dawla*, Casablanca, 1981, ch. iv.

[59] Bukhari, Book 56, Hadith 108.

[60] See Lewis, Bernard, "The State and the Individual in Islamic Society," paper delivered at the *International Symposium on the Moral and Political Vision of Islam*, Unesco, Paris, 7–10 Dec. 1982 (Multh.), p. 6.

[61] Cited in Gibb, H. A. R., *op. cit.*, p. 15.

in his individual capacity and autonomy, in the sphere of "civil" rights, even *vis-à-vis* the state itself.[62]

Other factors sustaining individualism in classical Islam can be found in the *Sufi* movements and their individualistic mystical approach to religious truth.[63] A *Sufi* is indeed an "outwordly individual," similar in many respects to the Indian renouncer studies by Dumont.[64] Yet, Sufism was not an "outwordly movement" given the considerable influence it came to exercise upon many of the elements of Islamic civilisation. The place given to "Reason" in the enquiries of the *Falasifat*[65] along with that of "Free Will" in the works of the *Qadariyyun* and the *Mu'tazilah*[66] also contributed to enhance the worth of man in his independence and thereby of individualism.

In an attempt to sum up the situation of the individual, let us stress again that although Islam became a controlling system weakening blood and kinship bonds, the latter maintained much of the vitality so as to form with the universal and transcendent message of the new faith the two poles of a pervasive tension all through Islamic history.[67] The perspective offered by Islam for liberating the individual from his traditional ties was thus only partially accomplished. Under Islam, the value attached to the unity and cohesiveness of the *Umma* also impeded the full development of the individual. It remains true, however, that the recognition by Islam of the moral uniqueness of man, of his individual responsibility and of the sanctity of his "civil" rights, together with the inherited interest from Arab antiquity in personality and character and the influence of ideas such as those of the *Sufi(s)*, the *Mu'tazilah*, and the *Falasifat*, all formed conditions leading to the emergence of the autonomous and independent individual that citizenship presupposes.

The Question of Equality

It was noted earlier that individual citizens by virtue of their common status are characterised by their equality before the law. Here, the

---

[62] For example, "strictly speaking," observes Schacht, the state has neither Eminent Domain over public property, nor the confiscation of private property is "in principle" recognised. In addition, "the state is not privileged with regard to contracts and jurisdiction"; Schacht, Joseph, *op. cit.*, at 144, 141 and 142 respectively.

[63] Generally, see, Anawati, G. C. and Gardet, L., *Mystique musulmane*, Paris, 1961; Nicholson, R. A., *Studies in Islamic Mysticism*, Cambridge, 1971; and Schimmel, A. M., *Mystical dimensions of Islam*, Chapel Hill, 1975.

[64] See note 22, *supra*. For Dumont, the Indian renouncer becomes independent autonomous—i.e., an individual—by leaving the society; he is an "outwordly individual." In contrast, the "inwordly individual" lives in society, "in the world." On this opposition, see "Homo Hierarchicus" *op. cit.*, App. B.

[65] Generally see, Corbin, Henri, *Historie de la philosophie islamique*, Paris, 1964 and Fakhry, Majid, *A History of Islamic Philosophy*, 2nd edn., London, 1983.

[66] Generally see, Fakhry, Majid, "Some Paradoxical Implications of the Mutazilite View of Free Will" in *Muslim World*, 1953, pp. 98–108; and Watt, W. M., *Free Will and Predestination in Early Islam*, London, 1948.

[67] See note 26, *supra*.

development of the notion of citizenship could draw on the egalitarian principles underlined in Islam. However, as suggested by Gardet, two different types of equality ought first, to be discerned:[68] the equality of all human beings based on their human nature as God-made creatures of *tin* (clay) which conferred on them no rights and which remained a "negative equality"; and the equality of the believers, as brothers in *din* (religion) expressed in the Koranic verse: "All believers are but brethren"[69] and further stressed in the Prophet's *Hadith*: "People are equal as are the teeth of a comb. There is no merit for an Arab or a non-Arab; merit is by piety."[70] It is a "positive equality" entitling the believers to the rights with which their common status as members of the *Umma* is endowed. Thus, within the *Umma*, distinctions based on rank, wealth, kinship or race were not recognised: "The noblest amongst you is the most God-fearing," says the Koran.[71]

But all non-Moslems living in *Dar al-Islam* (the territory of the Islamic state) remained *without* the *Umma* and could neither acquire the "equal status" of its members nor enjoy their "equal rights." However, it is a double *contre sens* to qualify—as often found in orientalists' work—the situation of the *Dhimmi(s)*[72] as that of "second class" citizenship. First, because classical Islam, strictly speaking, did not know citizenship.[73] Second, because the *Umma*, as a political community, being exclusively based on *jus religionis*,[74] the *Dhimmi(s)* did not qualify for membership.[75] They could

---

[68] See Gardet, Louis, *op. cit.*, p. 51 and f. I borrow from him the opposition between "brothern in *tin*" and "brothern in *din*" and the subsequent one between "negative" and "positive" equalities. Generally on Islam as an egalitarian doctrine, see also Rabbath, Edmond, "La Théorie des Droits de L'Homme dans le Droit Musulman" in *Revue Internationale de Droit Comparé*, Vol. 11, Janv.—Mars 1959, pp. 653–72.

[69] Koran (49, 10).

[70] Ahmad Ibn Hanbal, *Al Musnad, op. cit*, Vol. 6, p. 411.

[71] Koran (49, 13).

[72] On the question of *Dhimmi(s)*, generally see Cahen, Claude, "l'Islam et les minorite's confessionelles au cours de l'histoire" in *La Tables Ronde*, no 126, Juin 1958, pp. 61–72; and *idem*, "Dhimma" in *Encyclopaedia of Islam*, 2nd edn. (hereafter cited as E.I.2).

[73] Employing the term "citizen" with reference to classical Islam, a usage which is found in the works of authors such as H. A. R. Gibb, M. Hodgson and E. Rabbath, is imprecise and possibly also misleading.

[74] As distinguished from *jus sanguini* as opposed to *jus soli*.

[75] This is unless they responded to the appeal of Islam and converted to the new religion which was an option followed by only few amongst them, indeed. The maintenance however of such a possibility at all times renders trivial comparing, the situation under Islam to the caste system in India or the freemen criterion for membership in the Greek *polis*, both characterised by their impermeability. Inasmuch as "comparisons" are deemed useful, the situation for the *Dhimmi(s)* could be better understood, *mutatis mutandis*, by analogy to modern differences between the rights of "nationals' and resident foreigners" rather than by analogy to inequalities related to citizenship, whether ancient or modern, or to caste distinctions.

not, accordingly, enjoy the same rights as those accorded to Muslims, but neither were they obligated by the same duties.[76]

Finally, in spite of the fact that within the *Umma* as well, Islamic egalitarianism did not "equally" apply to slaves and women,[77] nor was the practice always in conformity with the general principles—as illustrated, for example, in the operation of the doctrine of *Kafa'a*[78]—there is no doubt that the high value which remained attached to the notion of equality in the Islamic tradition reflects the rootedness in Muslim minds of the idea itself as a form of justice.[79] It also represents the permanence of an aspiration whose contemporary expression can best be found in the quest for full citizenship.

The Problem of Political Participation

A major factor, however, was to impede the development of the idea of citizenship down to the late Ottoman days. It is the limit imposed by the very nature of *Shari'a* itself on the possibility and scope of "participation." God Himself being the supreme sovereign and the sole legislator in Islam,[80]

> . . . there can be "no sovereign state," in the sense that the state has the right of enacting its own laws, although it may have some freedom in determining its constitutional structure. The Law precedes the state, both logically and in terms of time; and the state exists for the sole purpose of maintaining and enforcing the law.[81]

---

[76] Relevant here to how *jus religionis* affected the definition of duties is Gibb's observation that "patriotism in the political or geographical sense is irrelevant, apostasy is the equivalent of treason and is punished with death: Gibb, H. A. R., *op. cit.*, p. 14.

[77] In addition to the legal incapacities and aspects of Family law often cited to that effect, differences in amounts of due *Diya*, i.e., compensation payable in cases of homicide, are even more pertinent for they reflect unequal judgments of "worth," generally see article "*Diya*," in *E.I.2* and for illustration, Ibn Qudama, *Al Mughni wa-l sharh al-Kabir*, Vol. 9, Beirut, 1983, pp. 480–671.

[78] Article "Kafa'a" in *E.I.2* defines the notion in the following terms: "In the terminology of *fikh* [Kafa'a] designates equivalence of social status, fortune and profession (those followed by the husband and by the father-in-law), as well as parity of birth, which should exist between husband and wife in default of which the marriage is considered ill-matched and in consequence, liable to break-up. In fact, in *fikh kafa'a* works in a single direction and protects only the wife who must not marry beneath her." On the subject, see generally Ziadeh, Farhat J., "Equality (Kafa'ah) in the Muslim law of Marriage" in *The American Journal of Comparative Law*, Vol. VI. 1957, 1–4, pp. 503–17; and Linant De Bellefonds, Y., *Traité de Droit Musulman Comparé*, Paris, 1965, Vol. 2 pp. 171–81; on how profession could become a source of social discrimination and inequality of treatment see Brunschvig, Robert, "Mètiers vils en Islam" in his collection of articles, *Etudes d'Islamologie*, Vol.1, Paris, 1976, pp. 145–64.

[79] Generally see, Khadduri, Majid, *The Islamic Conception of Justice*, Baltimore, 1984.

[80] "Knowest you not that to God belongs the Kingdom of the heavens and the earth, and that you have none, apart from God, neither protector nor helper?" and "Say, 'O God, Lord of all dominion! Thou grantest dominion unto whom Thou willest, and takest away dominion from whom Thou willest; and Thou exaltest whom Thou willest and abasest whom Thou willest. In Thy hand is all good. Verily, Thou has the power to will anything,'" says the Koran (2, 107) and (3, 26), respectively.

[81] Gibb, H. A. R., *op. cit.*, p. 3.

And it is only from the divine law that political authority could derive its legitimacy. Hence, "participation" operated in a very restricted sense and only in the limited instances of *bay'a* of the ruler (investiture)[82] and *shura* (consultation)[83] and in the formation of *ijma'* (consensus),[84] as a secondary source of law. Furthermore the "participatory" element embodied, in principle, in these practices—whose eventual beneficiaries were yet not all individuals but social and learned elites—became increasingly distorted, leading to its complete erosion over the years.

In conclusion to that section on the question of citizenship in classical Islam and by way of introduction to the great changes of the nineteenth century, we observe after Lewis how:

> . . . when ancient Greek political writings were translated into Arabic in the high Middle Ages, and served as the basis of a new and original political literature in Arabic, there was an equivalent for the city; there was none for the citizen. The Greek word *polis*, "city," was rendered as *Madina*, the Greek word *polites*, "citizen," found no true equivalent. . . . It was not until the general adoption of Western ideas of nationality and citizenship in the Islamic world that a term was needed and found.[85]

THE CHANGES IN MODERN OTTOMAN TIMES WHICH MADE CITIZENSHIP POSSIBLE

Nothing in Islamic history has had as powerful an impact on Muslim societies as their new encounter with the West beginning in the late eighteenth century. The challenges it posed and the efforts to respond to them have led to radical and widespread changes in these societies affecting their economic processes, their social structures, their political organisation, their legal system and above all their ideological views.[86]

---

[82] Generally see article "Bay'a" in *E.I.2*.

[83] Generally see article "*Mashwara*" in *E.I.2*.

[84] A good presentation of the question can still be found in Abdur Rahim, M. A., *The Principles of Muhammadan Jurisprudence*, London, 1911, pp. 115–36; see also article "Ijma'" in *E.I.2*.

[85] Lewis, Bernard, *The Political Language of Islam*, 1988, p. 63. We disagree however, with Lewis when he adds that "the word *Madani* by which [citizen was] usually translated, means something more like 'statesman.'" *Idem*. Rather, *Madani* conveyed the meaning of inhabitant of the city, the *citadin* (as distinguished from citizen); it was also used by Arab philosophers in the sense of "social being" (as distinguished from "political being").

[86] On the impact of the encounter and the challenges it posed, see generally, Gibb, H. A. R. and Bowen, Harold, *Islamic Society and the West*, Vol. I, London, Part 2, 1957; Hourani, Albert, *Arabic Thought in the Liberal Age 1789–1939*, Oxford, 1970: Issawi, Charles (ed.), *The Economic History of the Middle East 1800–1914*, Chicago, 1914; Lewis, Bernard, *The Emergence of Modern Turkey*, London, 1961; and Polk, William R. and Chambers, Richard L. (eds.), *Beginnings of Modernization in the Middle East*, Chicago, 1968.

The critical nature of these new challenges was made unmistakably clear by the defeats of the Ottomans before Russia and Austria, Napoleon's occupation of Egypt, and the later successes of the revolts in the Balkans. Hence, the first responses to them came in the form of an increased awareness of the need to reorganise the army on modern bases and to develop education—mainly as an attempt to master Western sciences and technology. The way was thus paved for the entry of new ideas and for the political and institutional reforms initiated under the Ottoman *Tanzimat* (1839–1876).[87]

First, military training schools with French instructors were opened and later organised educational missions were sent to Europe. In Istanbul, a translation bureau was established and French and Italian were taught in the new educational institutions. In these institutions no longer were only officers trained but also doctors, engineers, diplomats and civil servants. Similar modern educational institutions were to be established in Cairo, Beirut and Tunis as well. Throughout the nineteenth century contacts with Europe were to intensify due also to the increasing role played by Ottoman diplomatic missions in Europe and their counterparts in Istanbul and to the expansion of trade and the development of modern communication—which brought Europe even closer to Ottoman lands, especially with the introduction of steam boats in the Mediterranean sea and the later establishment of telegraphic lines. The number of missionary schools kept increasing as well, particularly in those parts of Lebanon, Palestine and Syria with significant Christian populations who in turn played a prominent role in the promotion of these contacts.[88]

However, most significant in these exchanges is not their unprecedented magnitude, but rather the fact that they were taking place at a moment of great changes in Europe and of intense ideological and political debates marked by the French revolution of 1789 and its ideas. As a matter of fact, with the movement of goods and people and the quest for acquiring modern skills, the Western ideas of these days were bound to enter Islamdom. Positivist and scientistic views along with the high values attached to efficiency and progress came with the modernisation of education; and the works of Voltaire, Montesquieu, Rousseau, Fenelon and Fontenelle were read and some of them translated by members of the emerging group of reformists in the Empire. The dissemination of these

---

[87] On the *Tanzimat*, generally see, Berkes, Niyazi, *The Development of Secularism in Turkey*, Montreal, 1964; Davison, Roderic H., *Essays in Ottoman and Turkish History, 1774–1923, The Impact of the West*, Austin, 1990; Engelhardt, Edward, *La Turquie et le Tanzimat*, 2 Vols., Paris, 1882–4; and Shaw, Stanford J. and Sharq, Ezel Kural, *History of the Ottoman Empire and Modern Turkey*, Vol. II, Cambridge, 1977.
[88] For all of this paragraph, see generally the works cited in note 77, *supra*.

new ideas was further made possible after 1840 by the advent of a Turkish press.[89]

First recognised for its "technological" superiority, then for its organisation, later the West became a source of inspiration in terms of ideas. According to Lewis, this was facilitated because "the French Revolution [was] the first great movement of ideas in Christendom which was not Christian but was even, in a sense, anti-Christian, and could therefore be considered by Muslim observers with relative detachment."[90]

However, the influence of Western ideas, particularly those of the French Revolution remained "composite."[91] Only selectively and after passing a test of "adaptability" were Western ideas drawn upon; the central issue being their conciliation with the principles of Islam and *Shari'a*.[92] Yet, over the years these efforts tended to reflect not one, but rather two, reinforcing processes: interpreting Western notions in a manner compatible with the *Shari'a* precepts; and re-interpreting the latter with the view of accommodating the needs generated by the challenges of the West.[93]

Focusing on the factors promoting the rise of the modern notion of citizenship in that area of radical transformation, we shall discuss three major changes together with the underlying ideological trends sustaining them: the expansion of equality under the *Tanzimat*; the establishment of "representative" and participatory" organs; and the adoption of the nationality principle.

The Expansion of Equality under the Tanzimat

The proclamation of the *Hatt-i Serif* of Gulhane of 3 November 1839, known as the Rescript of the Rose Chamber [94] is a landmark in the process

---

[89] In addition to Berkes, Niazi, *op. cit.*, Hourani, Albert, *op. cit.* and Lewis, Bernard, *op. cit.*, generally see Lewis, Bernard, "The Impact of the French Revolution on Turkey" in *Journal of World History*, Vol. 1, 1953, pp. 105–95; Mardin, Serif, *The Genesis of Young Ottoman Political Thought: A Study in the Modernization of Turkish Political Ideas*, Princeton, 1962; Mouvement Culturel—Antelias and Mouvement Culturel-France, ouvrage realisé par, *La Révolution Française el l'orient, 1789–1989*, Paris, 1990; and Revue Internationale des Sciences Sociales, *Influences de la Révolution Française*, no. special, 119/1989.

[90] Lewis, Bernard, "State and Society under Islam," in *The Wilson Quarterly*, Vol. 13, no. 6, Autumn 1989, p. 46.

[91] To use Bertrand Badie's term in his "L'impact de la Révolution Française sur les societes musulmanes. Evidence at Ambiguité," *op. cit.*

[92] Generally see Hourani, Albert, *op. cit.* and Mardin, Serif, *op. cit.*

[93] It should be noted here that "the Arabic-speaking Christians had not this problem, as observes Hourani, but a distinctive one of their own. Europe was not alien to them as it was to Muslims: in accepting its ideas and ways they need have no uneasy feeling of being untrue to themselves, or need to justify themselves to their fellows or their ancestors. But modern European thought was about rights and duties, about the nature and virtues of society: it posed questions to which, in their position as members of closed communities shut out of political life, there could be no answer." Hourani, Albert, *op. cit.*, p. 95.

[94] For the full text, see Hurewitz, J. C., *Diplomacy in the Near and Middle East: A Documentary Record*, Princeton, 1956, Vol. 2, pp. 113–16.

of "modernisation" of the Ottoman Empire, reflecting both the local desire to reorganise government and the pressures exerted by Western powers on the Empire. It declared the need for new institutions in order to carry out:

1. The guarantee ensuring to our subjects perfect security for life, honour and fortune.
2. A regular system of assessing and levying taxes.
3. An equally regular system for the levying of troops and the duration of the service.[95]

The edict clearly stated that "these imperial concessions shall extend to all our subjects, of whatever religion or sect they may be; they shall enjoy them without exception."[96] For the first time in Islamic history, Muslims and non-Muslims are deemed equal on the basis of a shared status, as subjects of the Sultan in this instance.

Traditionally, as "protected communities," the non-Muslims had enjoyed religious freedom and extensive autonomy in the conduct of their internal communal affairs; to a large degree they also had the same "civil rights" of individual Muslims, for example, in matters of contract and property.[97] However, they could not aspire—for reasons discussed earlier—to the equality of status reserved for the sole members of the *Umma*.[98]

The promises of the 1839 edict were not totally fulfilled. But as pressures from the Ottoman reformists on the one hand and from the European powers on the other kept mounting, a *Hatti-i Humayan*, an imperial rescript, was proclaimed on 18 February 1856.[99] It reaffirmed the principles laid down in the *Hatt-i Serif* and included more specific guarantees regarding the equal treatment of all Ottoman subjects in matters of taxation,[100] military service,[101] education,[102] and admissibility

---

[95] *Idem*, p. 114.

[96] *Idem*, p. 115.

[97] See note 71, *supra*.

[98] See note 74, *supra*.

[99] For the full text, see Hurewitz, J.C, *op. cit.*, pp. 149–53.

[100] "The taxes are to be levied under the same denomination from all the subjects of my Empire, without distinction of class or religion." *Idem*, p. 152.

[101] "The equality of taxes entailing equality of burdens, as equality of duties entail that of rights, Christian subjects, and those of other non-Mussulman sects, as it has been already decided, shall, as well as Mussulmans, be subject to the obligations of the law of recruitment." *Idem*.

[102] "All subjects of my Empire, without distinction, shall be received into the civil and military schools of the government if they otherwise satisfy the conditions as to age and examination which are specified in the organic regulations of the said schools." *Idem*, p. 151.

to public employment.[103] The prohibition of discrimination was also to cover "every distinction or designation tending to make any class whatever of the subject of my Empire inferior to another class, on account of their religion, language, or race."[104] The *Hatt-i Humayun* also promised that "the laws shall be put in force against the use of any injurious or offensive term, either among private individuals or on the part of the authorities."[105]

To fulfill the promises of the *Tanzimat* a fundamental contradiction in them still had to be resolved: for while "equality" was proclaimed, "separation" was also maintained; and the "privileges" of the non-Muslims to organise as distinct *millet(s)* were reaffirmed in the edicts.[106] The equality of the *Tanzimat* was also predicated on the shared status of "subjects of the Sultan" and not yet on that of common "membership" in the same political community, a development which would only occur at a later stage with the official adoption of the concept of Ottoman nationality.

However, at the time of the advent of the *Tanzimat*, the role of the national idea had come to play within the Ottoman Empire adversely affected the offered program of equality. "Many of the Christians wanted it to fail."[107] In fact, in Greece, Serbia, Roumania and Crete, Christians were no longer interested in equality within the Empire. Animated by a "nationalistic" spirit, they were rather seeking "autonomy" or secession and were advocating "independence." Apprehensive of the consequences the equality program may have on their ancestral prerogatives, the ecclesiastical hierarchies ruling over the Christian *millet(s)* were also opposed, seeing the project as one that would "both decrease their authority and lighten their purses."[108]

The *Tanzimat* were met with even greater opposition in the Islamic main body of the empire. For the more conservative elements of the *Ulama'* (religious scholars) establishment, such a program of equality was a mere *bid'a* (innovation).[109] To the popular mind, the differentiated status of Muslims remained to be perceived as a legitimate consequence of their superiority in the possession of Truth, which neither the Christians nor the Jews could attain because it was only fully revealed in the Koranic

---

[103] "The nomination and choice of all functionaries and other employees of my Empire being wholly dependent upon my sovereign will, all the subjects of my Empire, without distinction of nationality, shall be admissible to public employment and qualified to fill them according to their capacity and merit, and comfortably with rules to be generally applied." *Idem.*

[104] *Idem.*

[105] *Idem.*

[106] *Idem.*

[107] Davison, Roderic H., *op. cit.*, p. 111.

[108] *Idem.*

[109] Used here in the sense of *bid'a madhmuma* (erring innovation and thus blameworthy) as opposed to a *bid'a mahmuda* (praiseworthy). See generally article *"Bid'a"* in *E.I.2.*

message.[110] Finally, to the new generation of Ottoman reformists, the "New Ottomans," the *Tanzimat*—particularly in their enumeration of the privileges of the Christians as in the *Hatt-i Humayun* were seen as unjustified concessions granted in response to pressures exerted by the European powers on the Porte. "This, in the New Ottoman view, led to inequality, not equality."[111] For them foreign intervention should be resisted and equality based on a new bond of "Ottoman patriotism" and on the establishment of a "constitutional government."[112]

The Adoption of the Nationality Principle

Early expressions of the idea of *Osmanlilik*, or Ottomanism, can be found in the *Tanzimat*. The *Hatt-i Serif* of 1839 speaks of the "members of the Ottoman society"[113] and the *Hatt-i Humayun* of 1856 mentions the "cordial ties of patriotism"[114] uniting the subjects of the Empire. But the notion of Ottoman nationality, as criterion for membership in the Ottoman state, was officially adopted only at a later stage by the promulgation of the 1869 law on Ottoman nationality.[115] Adoption of the Ottoman nationality is confirmed in Article 7 of the 1876 Constitution:

> All subjects of the Empire are called Ottomans, without distinction, whatever faith they profess; the status of an Ottoman is acquired and lost, according to conditions specified by law.[116]

Although *Osmanlilik* was in line with the reformist spirit underlying the *Tanzimat*, it developed in part in reaction to the orientation followed by those edicts. *Osmanlilik* meant to convey the idea of a common tie both more fundamental than, and transcending of, the *millet* organisation which was left untouched—or rather reaffirmed—in the earlier *Tanzimat*.

Osmanlilik was intended to salvage the unity of an empire then threatened by upheavals from within its borders as much as from European interventions. It attempted to convey an idea of patriotism based on brotherhood and equality. The encounter with the West, however, had generated new contradictions and profound modifications in the relationships of social forces and the organisation of the economy: traditional

---

[110] Davison, Roderic H., *op. cit.*, pp. 120 and 121; for the threat the *Tanzimat*(s) posed to the prevailing political and social orders, see generally Hourani, Albert, "Ottoman Reform and the Politics of Notables" in Polk, William R. and Chambers, Richard L., *op. cit.*, pp. 41–68.
[111] Davison, Roderic H., *op. cit.*, p. 126.
[112] Generally see, Mardin, Serif, *op. cit.*, and Berkes, Niyazi, *op. cit.*
[113] See Hurewitz, J. C., *op. cit.*, p. 114.
[114] *Idem*, p. 150.
[115] Text in Young, George, *Corps de Droit Ottoman*, Oxford, 1905, Vol. II, pp. 226–29.
[116] Text in Hertslet, C. B. (Sir Edward), *The Map of Europe by Treaty*, London, 1891, Vol. IV, pp. 2531–40; see p. 2534.

forces were losing power while new ones were emerging and reaping most of the benefits from these changes. *Osmanlilik,* here, proved unable to prevent the crystallisation of these new tensions in violent confrontations opposing Moslems to Christians—now associated with the West's growing power—as in Damascus, Mount Lebanon and Aleppo. It failed also to halt both the continuing breaking away of the European provinces of the Empire and the increasing autonomy acquired by Arab provinces like Egypt and Tunisia.[117]

In its promotion of Ottoman patriotism, *Osmanlilik* officially recognised the territorial factor as constitutive of common identity. It came however at a time when other expressions of territorial patriotisms were also emerging within the Empire. In Egypt, Tahtawi, inspired by the meanings given to the concept of *patrie* in post-1789 France, started using the terms *watan* and *hubb al-watan* (love of country) in a new sense conveying the idea of territorial patriotism. In his writings, the notion of *watan* was clearly distinguished from that of *Umma*. It referred to Egypt as a focus of identity and duties. This, however, was not exclusive of the maintained sense of loyalty to the *Umma* because of the territorial nature of the idea of *watan*.[118] In Lebanon, for Butrus al Bustani, the prominent Christian scholar and publicist, Syria gradually became the object of a comparable type of territorial patriotism.[119]

Irrespective of what was going to be the fate of *Osmanlilik,* its role in the development of citizenship remains of prime importance. With its introduction of the territorial factor, the nature of the political community was bound to change. Moslems and non-Moslems are thus deemed equal, no longer as "subjects" of the Sultan only, but by the fact of their common membership in the political community. And equality in rights becomes an attribute of the new-shared status. Article 18 of the 1876 Ottoman Constitution reads:

> All *Ottomans* are equal in the eye of the law. They have the same rights and owe the same duties towards their country, without prejudice to religion.[120]

In view of their territorial nature, Egyptian and Syrian patriotisms played a similar role in laying the groundwork for the emergence of the idea of

---

[117] See generally, Anderson, M. S., *The Eastern Question 1774–1923: a Study in International Relations,* London, 1966; and Hourani, Albert, *A History of the Arab Peoples,* Cambridge, 1991, Part IV.

[118] On the changing meaning of *Watan,* see Lewis, Bernard, *op. cit.,* pp. 40–41 and 60–63; on Tahtawi see Hourani, Albert, *op. cit.,* p. 69 and f. An indication of Tahtawi's influence in his own times can be found in that his major work, *Takhlis al-ibriz fi talkhis Bariz,* first published in 1831, was reprinted three times during the nineteenth century.

[119] *Idem,* p. 99 and f.

[120] Hertslet, C. B. (Sir Edward), *op. cit.,* p. 2534 (emphasis added).

citizenship. However, *Osmanlilik* and the other forms of territorial patriotism were to be transformed by the power that the national idea and the
new forces of nationalism were gaining within the Empire. Thus, at the
dawn of the First World War, we will find the emerging—but unequally
developed—Turkish, Arab, Syrian, Egyptian and Lebanese "nationalisms"
to be competing.[121]

And with the success of the national idea, the concept of citizenship
appears to be making another breakthrough owing to the further decline
of the religious criterion and the adoption of the linguistic criterion, in
addition to the territorial, as grounds for membership in the political
community.

The Question of Representation and Constitutionalism

Citizenship, it has been said, presupposes that the political community is
considered to form a body vested with sovereignty; from this, citizens'
"participatory" rights are derived. Under Ottoman rule, however, it is the
development of the idea of "participation," stimulated by the creation of
"representative" organs, that gradually led to the redefinition of the
notion of sovereignty. This could be explained on the ground that the new
"representative" and "participatory" institutions could be justified—not
without difficulty, however—as conforming with traditional Islamic practices such as *shura*, while the introduction of the concept of "popular
sovereignty" posed a much greater obstacle, sovereignty being in the
traditional view—as seen earlier—an attribute of God, solely.

The roots of representative government are to be found in the *Tanzimat*.
Its first manifestations were the 1840 Firman calling on provincial officials
to establish "administrative councils" and the convocation in 1845 of an
extraordinary "assembly" in Istanbul.[122] The representative principle was
expanded in the 1856 *Hatt-i Humayun* which provided that measures be
taken to reform the "provincial and administrative councils" in order to
"ensure fairness in the choice of the deputies of the Mussulman, Christian,
and other communities and [ensure] freedom of voting,"[123] that the
"temporal administration" of the non-Muslim communities "be placed

---

[121] See generally Antonius, George, *The Arab Awakening: The Story of the Arab Nationalist Movement*, London, 1938; Hourani, Albert, *op. cit.*, chs. VIII and IX; and Lewis, Bernard, *op. cit.*,
chs. VI and VIII.

[122] See Davison, Roderic H., *op cit.*, pp. 101–2. It is noteworthy to mention here that a decade
before the 1840 firman, a system of local councils had been established in Syria and
Palestine, then under the rule of Muhammad Ali of Egypt. On the subject, see Ma'oz, Moshe,
"The balance of power in the Syrian town during the Tanzimat period, 1840–61" in *Bulletin
of the School of Oriental and African Studies, University of London*, Vol. XXIX, Part 2, 1966,
pp. 277–301.

[123] See Hurewitz, J. C., *op cit.*, p. 152.

under the safeguards of an assembly to be chosen from among the members both ecclesiastical and layman of the said communities,"[124] and that "the heads of each community and a delegate designated by the Sublime Porte [participate] in the deliberations of the Supreme Counsel of Justice on all occasions which might interest the generality of the subjects of my Empire."[125]

The Vilayet Law of 1864 confirmed the adoption of the representative principle. But this was still an indirect and a *millet*-based system of representation.[126] Moreover, remarks Davison:

> . . . all the institutions worked imperfectly, some very poorly indeed, and the representative principle was more often breached than observed. No one could maintain that the common people of the Empire were generally represented, or that such elections as existed were not as a rule tightly controlled by officials or local notables.[127]

But Davison also correctly adds that "the representative principle was, in several ways, firmly embedded in Ottoman law."[128]

However, the mere establishment of representative organs could no longer satisfy the Ottoman reformists who were becoming increasingly influenced by European institutions and political processes. It only further stimulated their demands for more radical changes. The representative principle accepted, they now sought the creation of a parliament and the adoption of a constitutional form of government. Europe's causes of strength and progress were no longer believed to derive mainly from its scientific and technological superiority, but rather from the nature of its political institutions—namely, parliaments, responsible ministers, and freedom of the press. Pioneering in the articulation of such new views and in the call for the adoption of European types of institutions was the Tunisian Khayr al-Din,[129] the author of *Aqwam al-Masalik Fi Ma'rifat Ahwal Al Mamalik*,[130] who played a prominent role in drafting the Tunisian Constitution of 1861, the first modern constitution to be promulgated under Islamic rule.

In Istanbul, the reformist Sinasi translated and published as a serial Vattel's *Le Droit des gens*, familiarising his readers thus with the notion of "natural rights." Shortly thereafter, another serial depicting the European

---

[124] *Idem*, p. 151.

[125] *Idem*, p. 153.

[126] For the text, see Young, George, *op. cit.*, Vol. I, pp. 36–45.

[127] See Davison, Roderic H., *op. cit.*, p. 105.

[128] *Idem*.

[129] See Brown, Leon Carl, *The Surest Path, the Political Treatise of a Nineteenth Century Muslim Statesman*, Cambridge, 1967 and generally Hourani, Albert, *op. cit.*, p. 86 and f.

[130] First published in Tunisia in 1867.

parliamentary system was to follow. Through Sinasi's journalistic contributions, new terms came to be introduced in the local political language such as citizen's rights, public opinion, constitutional government and natural rights of the people.[131]

Namik Kemal, the boldest of the new Ottoman ideologists, still insisted on "legitimising" his promotion of Western ideas and concepts as being natural developments from traditional Islamic notions and practices. Yet, in reality, his was a wholly new way of thinking in Islam.[132] Thus, while Islamic tradition granted the ruler quasi-legislative powers, through the recognised practice of *Siyasa*, for Kemal, "consultation" (*meshwerat* or *shura*) was seen as necessary in order "to keep the government within the limits of justice" and required that "the legislative power [be] taken away from the government," and placed in the exclusive possession of an elected assembly.[133] Even more radical was his argument about vesting the people with sovereignty:

> . . . the sovereignty of the people (*Hakimiyyet-i ahali*), which means that the powers of the government derive from the people and which in the language of the *Shari'a* is called *bay'a* . . . is the right necessarily arising from the personal independence (*Istiklal-i dhati*) that each individual by nature possesses.[134]

The influence of such new ideas coupled with the mounting political pressures on the Sultan led to the promulgation of the 1876 Constitution and its provision for an elected chamber of deputies.[135] In spite of the limited powers it was granted under the Constitution,[136] "the very existence of a Parliament must be viewed as a tremendous advance in the Ottoman political theory; for even impotent as it was, it still represented a recognition of the people's right to participate in government."[137]

In addition to being a landmark in the history of "participation," the new chamber played a critical role in changing the basis followed for representation. One of the most important bills it passed was the new electoral law which departed from the *millet* system in favour of an individual-based system which took no account of religious affiliation; an amendment to the bill providing for a fixed ratio of Muslim and non-Muslim deputies was defeated.[138]

---

[131] On Sinasi, see Mardin, Serif, *op. cit.*, pp. 252–75.

[132] On Namik Kemal, see *Idem*, pp. 283–336.

[133] Quoted in Lewis, Bernard, "Hurriyya" in *E.I.2*, Vol. 3, p. 592.

[134] *Idem*.

[135] Articles 65–80.

[136] For a discussion of the powers granted to Parliament under the 1876 Constitution, see Devereux, Robert, *The First Ottoman Constitutional Period: A Study of the Midhat Constitution and Parliament*, Baltimore, 1963, pp. 63–73.

[137] *Idem*, p. 70.

[138] *Idem*, p. 208.

The past Ottoman constitutional experience was short-lived. The Sultan suspended the Constitution in 1878 for 30 years and did not promulgate the new electoral law. But the Constitution was restored in 1908 and the electoral law was resurrected and served for the election of the second parliament of the Empire.

CONCLUSION

Starting in the mid-nineteenth century, the notion of citizenship was thus making a breakthrough in Islamdom owing to the influence Western ideas have had on the organisation and "modernisation" of the institutions and mode of government of the Ottoman Empire, and on the emergence of new trends of thought. It could also draw on the elements of individualism that had survived the classical period of Islam and on the egalitarianism of Islamic ideology. Its claim for legitimacy was associated with the attempts to revive the "participatory" elements originally existing in practices such as *bay'a*, *shura* and *ijma'* and their liberal interpretation in a way capable of accommodating the changes of modern times.

But the effects of the encounter with the West did not all point in a direction favourable to the full development of citizenship. Rather, they were to generate conflicting trends. We have seen how the *Tanzimat*'s position on equality embodied a contradiction, how *Osmanlilik* could not prevent the rise of antagonisms often leading to violent confrontations, and how fragile the constitutional experience was.

At the roots of these problems are tensions and dilemmas which reflected on the basic components of citizenship; the individual, the state, and the nature of the relationship existing between them.

As to the situation of the individual, the impact of the West, no doubt, created conditions bound to facilitate the processes of individuation and the weakening of "primary ties"; namely, the spread of modern education and its extension to women, the acceleration of urbanisation, the dissemination of new ideas about liberty and equality and the emphases on values such as rationality and progress. But the encounter with the West also sharpened religious cleavages, increased the militancy of minorities and stimulated traditional loyalties—through giving them new meanings.

While religion, family and clan gave the individual a "feeling of security and belonging,"[139] the new social and political conditions on which

---

[139] Fromm, Eric, *Escape from Freedom*, New York, 1965 edition, p. 58. "In having a distinct, unchangeable and unquestionable place in the social world from the moment of birth, adds Fromm, man was rooted in a structuralised whole and thus life had a meaning which left no place and no need for doubt." *Idem*.

the processes of individuation depended did not offer an unequivocal basis for the realisation of individuality. What happens in similar situations is that:

> ... powerful tendencies arise to escape from this kind of freedom [i.e., that which accompanies the processes of individuation] into submission or some kind of relationship to man and the world which promises relief from uncertainty, even if it deprives an individual of his freedom.[140]

It is true that "primary bonds once severed cannot be mended."[141] Still, the traditional frameworks of identity and solidarity could be vested with new meanings and reanimated under new forms. Hence the *millet(s)* organisation, for example, will provide a basis for new forms of political identification and solidarity and for the expression of nationalist types of aspirations. Another example, though on a different plane, can be found in the role the teachings of Shaykh Muhammed Abduh, the leading nineteenth century Muslim reformist, came to play. In his efforts to reconcile Islam with modern thought, Abduh rehabilitated the place of reason, called for breaking away from the method of *taqlid* (imitation) and reinstated the use of *ijtihad* (individual reasoning), thus enhancing the independence of the individual. Yet, his own teachings—and that of his disciple Rashid Rida[142]—when later interpreted with an emphasis on restoring the *Umma* will become a source of inspiration for the more militant Islamic movements.

This is to show that the impact of the West faced the individual with a dilemma, for it opened up to him two courses. In one, he could pursue, through political effort, the realisation of his increasing individuation into full citizenship. In the other, he could "fall back, or give up his freedom, and . . . try to overcome his aloneness by eliminating the gap that has arisen between his individual self and the world."[143] It is a course of "escape . . . characterized by the more or less complete surrender of individuality"[144]—be it in favour of a confessional group, a nationalistic movement, or a religious ideal.

With respect to the State, although the "territorial" principle became well established, the question of citizenship was also to be affected by the issues of delineating the boundaries of the political community and

---

[140] *Idem*, p. 52.

[141] *Idem*.

[142] On Abduh and Rida, generally see Hourani, Albert, *op. cit.*, pp. 130–60 and 222, 244; Kedourie, Elie, *Afghani and Abduh*, New York, 1966; and Kerr, Malcolm, *Islamic Reform: the Political and Legal Theories of Muhamad Abduh and Rashid Rida*, Berkeley, 1966.

[143] Fromm, Eric, *op. cit.*, p. 161.

[144] *Idem*, p. 162.

establishing criteria for its membership—both of which remained disputed questions. Here, in addition to the previously mentioned emergence of competing forms of nationalisms, the problem was further complicated by two factors. First, the aftermath of the First World War, most of the newly formed states which were to succeed the Ottoman Empire were perceived as Western creations—or better, as an outcome of imperialistic designs. This not only generally impinged on their quest for legitimacy, it also led certain sectors of their populations to challenge the "citizenship status" they were being offered with these entities because of its connections to the establishment of a "nationality" tie which they opposed. Second, some of these states were formed around, and came to be dominated by, certain communal grounds such as religious confessions and extended families. In practice, this undermined the equality presupposed by the citizenship status, even though its principle was recognised in the laws and constitutions of these states. Different classes of "citizens," with different rights, were in fact to take form, thus distorting the concept of citizenship itself.

Finally, as "participation" became increasingly associated with "constitutionalism" and "parliamentary democracy," its fate was affected both by changes in Western attitudes and changes in Arab and Moslem attitudes *vis-à-vis* the West. As to the former, the West—as noted earlier—had encouraged the establishment of "representative" and "participatory" institutions in the Ottoman Empire. But when after the First World War France and Britain came to assume direct responsibility in the Arab provinces of the defunct Empire, although they provided them in most instances with modern constitutions and parliamentary types of institutions their practice was rather one of manipulated elections and suspended constitutions. During the period between World War One and World War Two mainstream Arab and Moslem attitudes *vis-à-vis* the West were also changing. Western nations were less perceived to form models to imitate and more considered to represent imperialistic powers. Feelings of hostility *vis-à-vis* the West increased though its original attraction never totally disappeared. In the wake of these changes, Western types of institutions and democracy came to be rejected as alien and deceptive. "Participation" suffered but the idea of citizenship kept gaining roots and continues to express an unfulfilled quest in Arab and Moslem countries.

Notes

Introduction

1. Marshall G. S. Hodgson, *The Venture of Islam: Conscience and History in a World Civilization*, vol. 1: *The Classical Age of Islam* (Chicago and London: University of Chicago Press, 1974: 57).

Chapter 1

1. *Atatürk'ün Yazdigi Yurttaslik Bilgileri* (Citizen Information Written by Atatürk), ed. Nuran Tezcan (Istanbul: Çagdas Yayinlari, 1996: 54); trans. and quoted in Ayse Kadioglu, "Citizenship and Individuation in Turkey: The Triumph of Will over Reason," Cemoti 26, L'individu en Turquie et en Iran [En ligne] (20 mars 2006). (http://cemoti.revues.org/document34.html)

2. Fouad Ajami, *The Dream Palace of the Arabs: A Generation's Odyssey* (New York: Pantheon Books, 1998: 92).

3. Jalal Al-e Ahmad, *Gharbzadegi (Weststruckness)*, trans. John Green and Ahmad Alizadeh (Lexington, Kentucky: Mazda Publishers, 1982: 16).

4. See Augustus Richard Norton, "The Future of Civil Society in the Middle East," *Middle East Journal* 47 (Spring 1993: 211).

5. Ajami, *Dream Palace*, 61.

6. Curtis Harnack, *Persian Lions, Persian Lambs* (New York: Holt, Rinehart, and Winston, 1965: 42–46); redacted in Joseph S. Szyliowicz, *Education and Modernization in the Middle East* (Ithaca and London: Cornell University Press, 1973: 403–404).

7. Mohammed Reza Shah, *Mission for My Country* (New York: McGraw-Hill, 1961: 255); cited in Szyliowicz, *Education and Modernization in the Middle East*, 397.

Chapter 2

1. Because humanism exists today as a movement and a topic of controversy, some caution is necessary to differentiate its past from its present. Differences in terminology notwithstanding, it is probably safe to say that, in its emergent phase, the humanist mindset consisted of the tenets addressed here. A helpful source for sorting out the strands of the movement over time is the article "Humanism," *New Encyclopedia Britannica* (1992: 665–77). See also the list of books in Section 2.c of Further Readings in this work.

2. For a translated excerpt of the *Cronica*, see John Ruskin, *Val d'Arno: Ten Lectures on the Tuscan Art Directly Antecedent to the Florentine Year of Victories* (Sunnyside, Orpinton, Kent: G. Allen, 1874: Pt. 1, Lecture iii, Note 66).

3. Quotations and section references from *al-Muqaddima* follow Franz Rosenthal's *The Muqaddimah: An Introduction to History*, 3 vols. (New York: Pantheon Books, 1958), and N. J. Dawood's abridged edition (Princeton: Princeton University Press, 1969).

4. Marshall G. S. Hodgson, *The Venture of Islam: Conscience and History in a World Civilization*, vol. 2: *The Expansion of Islam in the Middle Periods* (Chicago and London: University of Chicago Press, 1974: 255).

5. *Ibid.*, 203.

6. Ira Lapidus, *Muslim Cities in the Later Middle Ages* (Cambridge: Harvard University Press, 1967: 108).

7. Fazlur Rahman, *Islam and Modernity: Transformation of an Intellectual Tradition* (Chicago; London: University of Chicago Press, 1984: 30).

8. J. Robson, "Bid'a," *Encyclopedia of Islam*, new ed., vol. 5, 1199.

Chapter 3

1. Excerpt from "To the Roman People, Urging Them to Intercede in Rienzo's Trial," English trans. in James Harvey Robinson, *Petrarch: The First Modern Scholar and Man of Letters* (Honolulu: University Press of the Pacific, 2004: 355–357).

2. Excerpt from "To Charles IV, Emperor August of the Romans," English trans. in *ibid.*, 365.

3. Excerpt from "Oration for the Funeral of Nanni Strozzi," English trans. in Gordon Griffiths, et al., *The Humanism of Leonardo Bruni: Selected Texts* (Binghamton, New York: The Renaissance Society of American, 1987: 125).

4. Excerpt from "Disclaim of Jealousy Toward Dante," English trans. in Robinson, *First Modern Scholar*, 183.

5. Even prior to the Renaissance, the jurists of Italy viewed the city as superior to the countryside. For further, see Peter N. Riesenberg, *Citizenship in the Western Tradition* (Chapel Hill: University of North Carolina Press, 1994: 158, 184).

6. English translations of the Qur'an are extracted or adapted from A. J. Arberry, *The Koran Interpreted* (London: Allen & Unwin; New York: MacMillan, 1955).

7. Sir Thomas W. Arnold, *The Caliphate* (Oxford: Clarendon Press, 1924: 49).

8. See John Kelsay, "Civil Society and Government in Islam" in Sohail H. Hashmi, *Islamic Political Ethics: Civil Society, Pluralism, and Conflict* (Princeton

and Oxford: Oxford University Press, 2002), 21–22. Within the present work, the topic of individualism is more broadly discussed in Part 2 of Nawaf Salam's article in the appendix, and the Islamic Modernist movement is discussed in Chapter 5.

9. A. K. S. Lambton, *State and Government in Medieval Islam: An Introduction to the Study of Islamic Political Theory* (Oxford; New York: Oxford University Press, 1981: xv).

10. H. A. R. Gibb and Harold Bowen, *Islamic Society and the West: The Study of the Impact of Western Civilization on Muslim Culture in the Near East* (London; New York: Oxford University Press, 1957: Vol. 1, Pt. 2, 212).

11. David Pryce-Jones, *The Closed Circle: An Interpretation of the Arabs* (Chicago: Ivan R. Dee, 2002: 99).

Chapter 4

1. Abul A'la Maududi, *A Short History of the Revivalist Movement in Islam*, trans. M. A. al-Ash'ari (Lahore: Islamic Publications Limited, 1963: 24–25).

2. Sayyid Qutb, *Social Justice in Islam*, trans. John B. Hardie (Washington, D.C.: American Council of Learned Societies, 1953: 139–141).

3. Ruhollah Khomeini, *Islam and Revolution: Writings and Declarations of Imam Khomeini*, translated by Hamdi Algar (Berkeley: Mizan Press, 1981: 75).

4. English translations vary. This incident is related in hadith 1509 of Bukhari's collection. The full English text is available from http://www.sunnipath.com/library.

5. See longer (translated) excerpt from Oruj's Tarîkh in P. M. Holt, et. al. (eds.). *Cambridge History of Islam*, vol. 1A (Cambridge, U.K.: Cambridge University Press, 1977: 270).

6. *Ibid.*, 290.

7. A. H. Nayyar and Ahmad Salim (eds.), *The Subtle Subversion: The State of Curriculum and Textbooks in Pakistan Urdu, English, Social Studies and Civics* (Islamabad: Sustainable Development Policy Institute, 2003: 88; primary source information on 86–90).

8. This is the character analysis of Amir Hasan Siddiqi, *Heroes of Islam*, pt. 2, 2nd ed. (Karachi: Jamiyat-ul-Falah, 1970: 83, 104–106, 134–136).

9. Pertinent survey information is found in Golnar Mehran, "A Shi'ite Curriculum to Serve the Islamic Cause," Chapter 3 in Eleanor Abdella Doumato and Gregory Starrett, *Teaching Islam: Textbooks and Religion in the Middle East* (Boulder, Colorado; London: Lynne Rienner Publishers, 2007: especially 57–66) and in Gil Aloni, *Revolutionary Messages in Elementary School Textbooks in Iran* (Jerusalem: Harry S. Truman Research Institute for the Advancement of Peace, Hebrew University, 2002: especially 55–81).

10. English translation of long excerpt and original source citations in Aloni, *Revolutionary Messages*, 69–70.

11. *Ibid.*, 66.

12. Seif Da'na, "A Conflict of Historical Narratives," Chapter 7a in Doumato, *Teaching Islam*, 144.

13. Excerpt as English translation is quoted in Kamran Scot Aghaie, *The Martyrs of Karbala: Shi'i Symbols and Rituals in Modern Iran* (Seattle: University of Washington Press, 2004: 134).

14. *Ibid.*, 138; the further value of this work is its collection of (unnumbered) full-color plates, which portray many aspects of Karbala rituals and memorialization of martyrdom.

15. Translated excerpt from "To Our Brothers in Pakistan," in Osama bin Laden, *Messages to the World: The Statements of Osama bin Laden*, ed. Bruce Lawrence, trans. James Howarth (London: New York: Verso, 2005: 101).

16. Ray, Arjun, *Kashmir Diary: Psychology of Militancy* (New Delhi: Manas Publications, 1997: 38–39).

17. Anne Marie Oliver and Paul Steinberg, *The Road to Martyr's Square: A Journey into the World of the Suicide Bomber* (New York: Oxford University Press, 2005: 62; for the two following quotations 65 and 71, respectively).

18. *Ibid.*, 84.

19. *Ibid.*, 121.

Chapter 5

1. Albert Hourani, *Arabic Thought in the Liberal Age, 1798–1939* (London; New York: Oxford University Press, 1970: 144).

2. Arturo Escobar, "The Invention of Development," *Current History* (November 1999: 384).

3. See Tu Wei-ming, ed., *Confucian Traditions in East Asian Modernity: Moral Education and Economic Culture in Japan and the Four Mini-Dragons* (Cambridge, MA: Harvard University Press, 1996).

4. See longer translated quote from 'Abduh in Fazlur Rahman, *Islam and Modernity: Transformation of an Intellectual Tradition* (Chicago: University of Chicago Press, 1984: 64).

5. Citation of relevant curriculum in Gil Aloni, *Revolutionary Messages in Elementary School Textbooks in Iran* (Jerusalem: Harry S. Truman Research Institute for the Advancement of Peace, Hebrew University, 2002: 65–68).

Glossary of Historical and Geographic Terms

Age of Revolution. Historic period from approximately 1750 to 1860 that encompassed the intellectual and political ferment that resulted in the American Revolution of 1775, the French Revolution of 1789, and the Central European revolts of 1848.

Anatolia. The peninsular land mass of Western Asia, bounded by the Mediterranean, Aegean, and Black Seas. The "Asia Minor" of the Romans, this area was a stronghold of the Byzantine (East Roman) Empire until it was overrun by Turkic tribes consequent to the Byzantine defeat at Manzikert in 1071 CE.

Andalus. The Arabic name for the Iberian Peninsula. The Muslim Arabs initially invaded that land in strength in 711 CE and advanced beyond the Pyrenees within two decades. Muslim rule in Spain was gradually eliminated consequent to the *Reconquista* (Christian reconquest); the last Muslim state (Granada) held out from 1236 to 1492 CE.

Arabistan. Geographic term vaguely designating the Arab-populated provinces of the Ottoman empire, encompassing present day Iraq, Syria, Lebanon, Israel–Palestine, Jordan, and parts of Arabia.

Caliph/caliphate. The office and the institution of the rulers who succeeded Muhammad as religious and governmental head of the Muslim community (*umma*) but without prophetic authority. The three Arab caliphal dynasties were the Rashidun, Rightly Guided (632–661 CE/11–40 AH); Umayyad (661–750 CE/41–132 AH); and Abbasid (750–1258 CE/132–656 AH).

Colonialism. A multiphase movement, extending from the fifteenth century to the early twentieth century, that entailed the European and (later) other imperialist subjugation of large parts of America, Asia, and Africa. After World War I, most of the Islamic world was under European (British, French, Italian, Dutch) control, either in colony, protectorate, or mandate status. The few exceptions were Afghanistan and the hinterland of Arabia, which were relatively inaccessible areas, and Turkey and Persia (Iran), which had to contend with foreign intervention. (See Chart on page xvi.)

Enlightenment. Philosophic movement in eighteenth-century Europe and America that occurred as one aspect of the Age of Reason. Enlightenment was the outcome of applying the principles of natural law theory, rationalism, and humanism in rethinking the subjects of ethics, metaphysics, epistemology, history, and socioeconomic and political philosophy.

Industrial Revolution. A trend spanning the late eighteenth and early nineteenth centuries in which there occurred major changes in agriculture, manufacturing, and transportation, first in Britain and then in other Western countries. The outcome was a significant transformation of material culture and socioeconomic conditions.

Islamic Conquests. Also known as Arab Conquests, these followed the Prophet's establishment of an Islamic state in western Arabia and occurred as a two-phased movement. The early conquests, which occurred from 633 to 645 CE (11–24 AH), included Arabia, Syria, Palestine, Egypt, Persia, Mesopotamia, and Armenia. The Umayyad conquests, which occurred mostly from 698 to 715 CE (79–96 AH) included North Africa, Spain, Transoxiana, and northern India.

Levant/Levantine. Geographic term vaguely designating the Eastern Mediterranean region: in its broadest sense, all the littoral lands; in its narrowest sense, the Syro–Palestinian coastal area.

Maghrib (Maghreb). The Arabic name for western North Africa, roughly corresponding to Morocco and western Algeria.

Middle East. See Near East.

Mughal Empire. Islamic state existing from 1526 to 1712 CE that at its height encompassed, in present-day terms, most of India and (West) Pakistan and eastern Afghanistan. The ruling dynasty originated with Babur, great-grandson of Timur-e Lang (Tamerlane), hence the name Mughal—Persian for Mongol. This empire had the largest population—estimated at 100 to 150 million—of any state in premodern times.

Near East. A vague geographic term designating the Balkan peninsula and the lands of the Levant—the Eastern Mediterranean Region. The term emerged in the nineteenth century consequent to European concerns over the break-up of the Ottoman Empire. Following World War I, the geostrategic focus of the Western world shifted eastward toward the petroleum-rich lands. That shift was reflected in the newer term "Middle East," which excluded the Balkans but took in the Arabian Peninsula, Iraq, and Iran. Further shift of focus occurred consequent to events in Afghanistan and Iran in 1979, and the term Southwest Asia (SWA) came into vogue. This newest term excludes Turkey, Egypt, and other Levantine countries but includes Afghanistan and Pakistan.

Reformation. A movement in Europe that started as an effort to stop certain malpractices within the Catholic Church and culminated in the fragmentation of Western Christendom. The Reformation began with Martin Luther's protest in 1517 and ended with the Peace of Westphalia in 1648.

Renaissance. A cultural movement that spanned roughly the fourteenth through the seventeenth centuries CE, beginning in Italy and later spreading to the rest of Europe. It altered the late Medieval mindset of Western European society and had wide-ranging consequences in many intellectual and artistic pursuits.

Ottoman Empire. Vast Islamic state existing from circa 1299 to 1922 that at its largest extent, in the fifteenth and sixteenth centuries, included the Balkans, part of the Danubian Basin, the southern Ukraine, Anatolia, some of the Caucasus, Mesopotamia, Syria–Palestine, the Red Sea coastal areas (both sides), Egypt, and the North African coastal lands as far as Morocco. (See map on page xv.) The eponymous founder of the Ottoman dynasty was Osman Bey, who led Turkic border raiders in campaigns against the Byzantines.

Safavid Empire. Islamic state existing from 1501/1502 to1722 CE that at its height encompassed, in present-day terms, all of Iran and Azerbaijan, much of Afghanistan and Iraq, and parts of other bordering countries. The ruling dynasty emerged from the Safaviyeh Sufi order of Azerbaijan and imposed Twelver Shi'ism as the official state religion.

Sindh. Historically, a region of the Indian sub-continent encompassing the lower Indus Valley; also a province of modern Pakistan.

Southwest Asia. See Near East.

Sultan/sultanate. The person/office representing supreme political authority in an Islamic state, as distinct from the caliph/caliphate, which had religious authority as well. The demise of the effective political power of the caliphate gave rise to the institution of sultanate.

Further Reading

CHAPTER 1: STATES WITHOUT "CITIZENS": THESIS

Modernization of the Islamic World

Atabaki, Touraj, and Erik J. Zurcher, *Men of Order: Authoritarian Modernization Under Ataturk and Reza Shah* (London: I. B. Taurus, 2004).

Banani, Amin, *The Modernization of Iran* (Stanford: Stanford University Press, 1961).

Cooke, Hedly Vicars, *Challenge and Response in the Middle East, the Quest for Prosperity, 1919–1951* (New York: Harper, 1952).

Davison, Roderic, *Reform in the Ottoman Empire, 1856–1876* (Princeton: Princeton University Press, 1963).

Fisher, Sidney Nettleton, *The Military in the Middle East: Problems in Society and Government* (Columbus: Ohio State University Press, 1963).

Gibb, H. A. R., and Harold Bowen, *Islamic Society and the West: The Study of the Impact of Western Civilization on Muslim Culture in the Near East*, 2 vols. (London: Oxford University Press, 1957).

Hourani, Albert, *Arabic Thought in the Liberation Age 1798–1939* (London: Oxford University Press, 1962, latest ed. reprint 1967).

Kedourie, Elie, and Sylvia G. Haim, eds., *Towards a Modern Iran: Studies in Thought, Politics, and Society* (Totawa, NY: Frank Cass, 1980).

Landen, Robert G., *The Emergence of the Modern Middle East: Selected Readings* (New York: Van Nostrand Reinhold, 1970).

Laqueur, Walter, ed., *The Middle East in Transition: Studies in Contemporary History* (New York: Praeger, 1958, latest ed. reprint 1971).

Lewis, Bernard, *The Emergence of Modern Turkey* (London: Oxford University Press, 1961, latest ed. 3rd ed. 2001).

Polk, William R., and Richard L. Chambers, eds., *Beginnings of Modernization in the Middle East* (Chicago and London: University of Chicago Press, 1968).

Smith, William Cantrell, *Islam in Modern History* (Princeton, NJ: Princeton University Press, 1957, latest ed. reprint 1977).

Szyliowicz, Joseph S., *Education and Modernization in the Middle East* (Ithaca: Cornell University Press, 1973).

Yapp, Malcolm E., ed., *Making of the Modern Near East, 1792–1923* (London: Longman, 1987).

Crisis of Islamic Society

Ahmad, Jalal Al-e, *Gharbzadegi (Weststruckness)*, John Green and Ahmad Alizadeh, trans. (Lexington, KY: Mazda Publishers, 1982); also Paul Sprachman, trans. (as *Plagued by the West*) (Delmor, NY: Center for Iranian Studies, Columbia University, 1982).

Ahmed, Akbar S., *Islam Under Siege: Living Dangerously in a Post-Honor World* (U.K.: Polity Press, 2003, 2004).

Ajami, Fouad, *The Dream Palace of the Arabs: A Generation's Odyssey* (New York: Pantheon Books, 1998).

Arjomand, Said Amir, ed., *From Nationalism to Revolutionary Islam* (Albany, NY: SUNY Press, 1984).

Gilsenan, Michael, *Recognizing Islam: Religion and Society in the Modern Middle East* (New York: Pantheon Books, 1982, latest ed. rev. ed. 2000).

Hoodbhoy, Pervez, *Muslims and Science: Religious Orthodoxy and the Struggle for Rationality* (Lahore: Vanguard, 1991).

Leiden, Carl, ed., *The Conflict of Traditionalism and Modernism in the Muslim Middle East* (Austin: University of Texas Press, 1968).

Lewis, Bernard, *What Went Wrong? Western Impact and Middle East Response* (Oxford: Oxford University Press, 2002).

Tibi, Bassam, *The Crises of Modern Islam: A Preindustrial Culture in the Scientific-Technological Age*, Judith von Sivers, trans. (Salt Lake City: University of Utah Press, 1988).

Yassine, Abdessalam, and Muhtar Holland, *The Muslim Mind on Trial: Divine Revelation Versus Secular Rationalism* (Iowa City, IA: Justice and Spirituality Publications, 2003).

CHAPTER 2: WORLDS TOGETHER, WORLDS APART: CULTURES IN HISTORY

Famous Savants and Their Mediterranean Milieu

Abulafia, David, *Mediterranean Encounters, Economic, Religious, Political, 1100–1550* (Aldershot, U.K.: Ashgate, 2000).

Azmeh, Aziz, *Ibn Khaldun: An Essay in Reinterpretation* (London: Frank Cass, 1982, latest ed. 2002).

Baali, Fuad, *The Science of Human Social Organization: Conflicting Views on Ibn Khaldun's (1332–1406) Ilm al-Umran* (Lewiston, NY: Edwin Mellen Press, 2005).

Baali, Fuad, and Ali Wardi, *Ibn Khaldun and Islamic Thought-Styles, a Social Perspective* (Boston: G. K. Hall, 1981).

Baron, Hans, *From Petrarch to Leonardo Bruni: Studies in Humanistic and Political Literature* (Chicago: University of Chicago Press, 1968).

Brett, Michael, *Ibn Khaldun and the Medieval Maghrib* (Brookfield, VT: Ashgate, 1989).

Chiat, Marilyn, and Kathryn L. Reyerson, *The Medieval Mediterranean: Cross-Cultural Contacts* (St. Cloud, MN: North Star Press, 1988).

Colish, Marcia L., *Medieval Foundations of the Western Intellectual Tradition, 400–1400* (New Haven: Yale University Press, 1997).

Enan, Mohammad Abdallah, *Ibn Khaldun, His Life and Work*, trans. (Lahore: Sh. Muhammad Ashraf, 1941, latest ed. reprint 1993).

Holloway-Calthrop, H. C., *Petrarch: His Life and Times* (New York: Cooper Square Publishers, 1972, latest ed. reprint 2006).

Imam, Syed Mohammad Amir, *Some Aspects of Ibn Khaldun's Socio-Political Analysis of History: A Critical Appreciation* (Karachi: Khurasan Islamic Research Center, 1978).

Kristeller, Paul Oskar, *Renaissance Thought and its Sources* (New York: Colombia University Press, 1979).

Lacoste, Yves, *Ibn Khaldun: The Birth of History and the Past of the Third World* (London: Verso, 1984).

Mahdi, Muhsin, *Ibn Khaldun's Philosophy of History: A Study in the Philosophic Foundation of the Science of Culture* (London: G. Allen and Unwin, 1957, latest ed. reprint 2007).

Mazzotta, Giuseppe, *The Worlds of Petrarch* (Durham: Duke University Press, 1993, latest ed. reprint 1999).

Mazzocco, Angelo, ed., *Interpretations of Renaissance Humanism* (Leiden: Brill, 2006).

Nakosteen, Mehdi, *History of Islamic Origins of Western Education, AD 800–1350* (Boulder: University of Colorado Press, 1964).

Nolhac, Pierre de, *Petrarch and the Ancient World* (Boston: Merrymount Press, 1907, latest ed. reprint 1977).

Robinson, James Harvey, *Petrarch: The First Modern Scholar and Man of Letters* (New York; London: G. P. Putnam's Sons, 1914, latest ed. new ed. 2003).

Saliba, George, *Islamic Science and the Making of the European Renaissance* (Cambridge, MA: MIT Press, 2007).

Orthodoxy in Islam

Ahmad, Zaid, *The Epistemology of Ibn Khaldun* (London; New York: Routledge, 2003).

Bello, Iysa A., *The Medieval Islamic Controversy Between Philosophy and Orthodoxy: Ijmâ' and Ta'wîl in the Conflict Between al-Ghazâlî and Ibn Rushd* (Leiden: E. J. Brill, 1989).

Berkey, Jonathan Porter, *The Formation of Islam: Religion and Society in the Near East, 600–1800* (New York: Cambridge University Press, 2003: Pts. 3 and 4 apply).

Dodge, Bayard, *Muslim Education in Medieval Times* (Washington, D.C.: Middle East Institute, 1962).

Ghazali, Abu Hamid Muhammad, *The Incoherence of the Philosophers*, Michael E. Marmura, trans. (Provo, UT: Brigham Young University Press, 1997, latest ed. rev ed. 2002).

Hodgson, Marshall G. S., *The Venture of Islam: Conscience and History in a World Civilization*, Vol. 2: *The Expansion of Islam in the Middle Periods* (Chicago: University of Chicago Press, 1974).

Ibn Taymiyya, Ahmad, *Ibn Taymiyya Against the Greek Logicians*, Wael B. Hallaq, trans. (Oxford: Clarendon Press, 1993).

Rosenthal, Franz, *Knowledge Triumphant: The Concept of Knowledge in Medieval Islam* (Leiden: Brill, 1970, latest ed. reprint 2007).

Safi, Omid, *The Politics of Knowledge in Premodern Islam: Negotiating Ideology and Religious Inquiry* (Chapel Hill: University of North Carolina Press, 2006).

Watt, W. Montgomery, *The Faith and Practice of al-Ghazâlî* (London: G. Allen and Unwin, 1953).

Zilfi, Madeleine C., *The Politics of Piety: The Ottoman Ulema in the Post Classical Age 1600–1800* (Minneapolis: Bibliotheca Islamic, 1988).

Humanism in the West

Baron, Hans, *In Search of Florentine Civic Humanism: Essays on the Transition from Medieval to Modern Thought* (Princeton: Princeton University Press, 1988).

Davies, Tony, *Humanism* (London: Routledge, 1997, latest ed. reprint 2007).

Dickens, Arthur Geoffrey, *The Age of Humanism and Reformation: Europe in the Fourteenth, Fifteenth, and Sixteenth Centuries* (Englewood Cliffs, NJ: Prentice-Hall, 1972).

Goodman, Anthony, and Angus MacKay, eds., *The Impact of Humanism on Western Europe* (New York: Longman, 1990).

Grassi, Ernesto, *Renaissance Humanism: Studies in Philosophy and Poetics* (Binghamton, NY: Medieval and Renaissance Texts and Studies, 1988).

Kraye, Jill, *The Cambridge Companion to Renaissance Humanism* (Cambridge, U.K.: Cambridge University Press, 1996, latest ed. reprint 1998).

Nauert, Charles G., *Humanism and the Culture of Renaissance Europe* (New York: Cambridge University Press, 1995, latest ed. 2006).

Southern, Richard W., *Scholastic Humanism and the Unification of Europe: Aims, Methods, and Places* (Oxford: Blackwell, 1994, 1995).

Trinkaus, Charles Edward, *The Scope of Renaissance Humanism* (Ann Arbor: University of Michigan Press, 1984).

CHAPTER 3: KINSMEN, NOT INDIVIDUALS: CONTRAST IN ETHICS

Tribalism and Islamic Society

Ahmed, Akbar S., and David M. Hart, eds., *Islam and Tribal Societies: From the Atlas to the Indus* (London: Routledge & Keegan Paul, 1984).

Baali, Fuad, *Society, State, and Urbanism: Ibn Khaldun's Sociological Thought* (Albany: SUNY Press, 1988).

Gellner, Ernest, *Concept of Kinship: And Other Essays on Anthropological Methods and Explanation* (New York: B. Blackwell, 1987).

Hardin, Russell, *One for All: the Logic of Group Conflict* (Princeton: Princeton University Press, 1995).

Harris, Christopher Charles, *Kinship* (Minneapolis: University of Minnesota Press, 1990).

Hart, David M., *Qabila: Tribal Profiles and Tribe-State Relations in Morocco and on the Afghanistan-Pakistan Frontier* (Amsterdam: Het Spinhuis, 2001).

Hughes, Austin L., *Evolution and Human Kinship* (New York: Oxford University Press, 1988).

Ibn Khaldun, Abd al-Rahman, *The Muqaddimah: An Introduction to History*, 3 vols. Franz Rosenthal, trans. (New York: Pantheon Books, 1958); N. J. Dawood, ed. and abr. (Princeton: Princeton University Press, 1969).

Khoury, Philip S., and Joseph Kostner, eds., *Tribes and State Formation in the Middle East* (Berkeley: University of California Press, 1990, 1991).

Parkins, Robert, *Kinship: An Introduction to Basic Concepts* (Oxford: Blackwell Publishers, 1997).

Ethics in Orthodox Islam

Ali, Syed Ameer, *The Ethics of Islam* (Dacca: Society for Pakistan Studies, 1969).

Donaldson, Dwight M., *Studies in Muslim Ethics* (London: S.P.C.K., 1953).

Fakhry, M., *Ethical Theories in Islam* (Leiden: E. J. Brill, 1991, 2nd ed. 1994).

Ghazali, Muhammad, *Muslim's Character* (*An American-English Translation of Muhammad al-Ghazali's Khuluq al-Muslim*, Mufti A. H. Usmani, trans. (Chicago: Kazi Publications, 1988, rev. ed. 2004).

Hourani, George F., *Reason and Tradition in Islamic Ethics* (London: Cambridge University Press, 1985).

Izutsu, Toshihiko, *Ethico-Religious Concepts in the Qur'an* (Montreal: McGill University Press, 1966, latest ed. reprint 2002).

Johansen, Baber, *Contingency in a Sacred Law: Legal and Ethical Norms in the Muslim fiqh* (Leiden: Brill, 1999).

Qusaim, Mohammad A., *Ethics of al Ghazali: The Composite Ethics of Islam* (Delmar, NY: Caravan Books, 1977).

Umaruddin, Muhammad, *The Ethical Philosophy of al-Ghazzali* (Pakistan: Aligarch Muslim University, 1962, latest ed. reprint 1982).

Citizenship and Western Society

Beiner, Ronald, *Theorizing Citizenship* (Albany: SUNY Press, 1995).

Bullock, Alan, *The Humanist Tradition in the West* (New York: Norton, 1985).

Dagger, Richard, *Civic Virtues: Rights, Citizenship, and Republican Liberalism* (New York: Oxford University Press, 1997).

Dynneson, Thomas L., *Civism: Cultivating Citizenship in European History* (New York: Peter Lang Pub., 2001).

Ehrenberg, John, *Civil Society: The Critical History of an Idea* (New York: New York University Press, 1999).

Gurevich, Aron, *The Origins of European Individualism*, Katharine Judelson, trans. (Oxford: Blackwell, 1995).

Heater, Derek, *A Brief History of Citizenship* (New York: University of New York Press, 2004).

Honshau, Iseult, *Civic Republicanism* (London: Routledge, 2002).

Pocock, J. G. A., *The Machiavellian Moment: Florentine Political Thought and the Atlantic Republican Tradition* (Prince: Princeton University Press, 1975, 2nd ed. 2003).

Riesenberg, Peter N., *Citizenship in the Western Tradition* (Chapel Hill: University of North Carolina Press, 1992, 1994).

Skinner, Quentin, *The Foundations of Modern Political Thought* (Cambridge, U.K.: Cambridge University Press, 1978).

CHAPTER 4: MUJAHIDEEN AND HERO-MARTYRS: IMAGERY OF ACTIVE VIRTUE

Islamic Heroism in History and Legend

Abedi, Mehdi, and Bary Lengenhausen, eds., *Jihad and Shahadat: Struggle and Martyrdom in Islam* (Houston: Institute of Research and Islamic Studies, 1986).

Aghaie, Kamran Scot, *The Martyrs of Karbala: Shi'i Symbols and Rituals in Modern Iran* (Seattle: University of Washington Press, 2004).

Cook, David, *Martyrdom in Islam* (New York: Cambridge University Press, 2007).

Edwards, David B., *Heroes of the Age: Moral Fault Lines on the Afghan Frontier* (Berkeley: University of California Press, 1996).

Ghadanfar, Mahmoud Ahmad, *Commanders of the Muslim Armies* (Riyadh: Dar-as-Salam Publishers, 2001).

Hyder, Syed Akbar, *Reliving Karbala: Martyrdom in South Asian Memory* (New York: Oxford University Press, 2006).

Khwaja, Jamil Ahmad, *Hundred Great Muslims* (Lahore: Ferozsons, 1971, latest ed. reprint 1987).

Knappert, Jan, *Islamic Legends: Histories of the Heroes, Saints, and Prophets of Islam*, 2 vols. (Leiden: Brill, 1985, 1997).

Renard, John, *Islam and the Heroic Image: Themes in Literature and the Visual Arts* (Columbia: University of South Carolina Press, 1993).

Siddiqi, Amir Hasan, *Heroes of Islam*, 2 pts. (Karachi: Jamiyat-ul-Falah, 1966, 2nd ed. 1970).

Sieny, Mahmoud Esma'il, *Heroes of Islam* (Riyadh: Dar-as-Salam Publishers, 2000).

Wasti, Syed Tanvir, *Lives of the Ottoman Sultans* (Karachi: Midway Book House, 1977).

Islamic Ideals and School Texts

Aloni, Gil, *Revolutionary Messages in Elementary School Textbooks in Iran* (Jerusalem: Harry S. Truman Research Institute for Peace, 2002).

Doumato, Eleanor Abdella, and Gregory Starrett, *Teaching Islam: Textbooks and Religion in the Middle East* (Boulder: Lynne Rienner Publishers, 2007).

Herrera, Linda, and Carlos Alberto Torres, *Cultures of Arab Schooling: Critical Ethnographies from Egypt* (Albany: SUNY Press, 2006).

Jalalzaid, Musa Khan, *The Crisis of Education in Pakistan: State, Education, and the Textbooks* (Lahore: al-Abbas International, 2005).

Massiales, Byron G., and Samir Ahmad Jarrar, *Arab Education in Transition: A Source Book* (New York: Garland Press, 1991).

Nayyar, A. H., and Ahmad Salim, eds., *The Subtle Subversion: The State of Curriculum and Textbooks in Pakistan Urdu, English, Social Studies and Civics* (Islamabad: Sustainable Development Policy Institute, 2003, 2005).

Rosser, Yvette Claire, *Islamization of Pakistani Social Studies Textbooks* (New Delhi: Rupa & Co., 2003).

Heroes of the "Streets" and Camps

Abrahamian, Ervand, *The Iranian Mujahidin* (New Haven, CT: Yale University Press, 1989).

Davis, Joyce M., *Martyrs: Innocence, Vengeance, and Despair in the Middle East* (New York: Palgrave MacMillan, 2004).

Khalili, Laleh, *Heroes and Martyrs of Palestine: The Politics of National Commemoration* (Cambridge, U.K.: Cambridge University Press, 2007).

Khosrokhavar, Farahad, *Suicide Bombers: Allah's New Martyrs*, David Macey, trans. (London: Pluto Press, 2005).

Makdisi, Ussama, and Paul A. Silverstein, eds., *Memory and Violence in the Middle East and North Africa* (Bloomington: Indiana University Press, 2006).

Oliver, Mary Anne, and Paul F. Steinberg, *The Road to Martyr's Square: A Journey into the World of the Suicide Bomber* (New York: Oxford University Press, 2005).

Ram, Haggay, *Myth and Mobilization in Revolutionary Iran: The Use of Friday Congregational Sermons* (Washington, D.C.: American University Press, 1994).

Victor, Barbara, *Army of Roses: Inside the World of Palestinian Women Suicide Bombers* (Emmaus, PA: Rodale Books, 2003).

CHAPTER 5: MODERNISM AND AUTHENTICITY: CRITIQUE OF ENDEAVORS

Islamic Modernist Thought

Abusulayman, Abdulhamid, *Crisis in the Muslim Mind*, Yusuf Talal Delorenzo, trans. (Herndon, VA: International Institute of Islamic Thought, 1993, latest ed. reprint 2004).

Arkoun, Mohammed, *Islam: To Reform or to Subvert?* (London: Saqi Books, 2006).

Berry, Donald L., *Islam and Modernity Through the Writings of Islamist Modernist Fazlur Rahman* (Lewiston, NY: Edwin Mellon Press, 2003).

Bowers, Michaelle, and Charles Kurzman, eds., *An Islamic Reformation?* (Lanham, MD: Lexington Books, 2004).

Cooper, John, et al., *Islam and Modernity: Muslim Intellectuals Respond* (London: I. B. Taurus & Co. Ltd., 1998; new ed. 2000).

Forward, Martin, *The Failure of Islamic Modernism?: Syed Ameer Ali's Interpretation of Islam* (Bern: Peter Lang, 1999).
Gibbs, H. A. R., *Modern Trends in Islam* (Chicago: University of Chicago Press, 1947, 1972).
Kassim, Husain, *Legitimizing Modernity in Islam: Muslim Modus Vivendi and Western Modernity* (Lewiston, NY: Edwin Mellon Press, 2005).
Kurzman, Charles, *Modernist Islam, 1840–1940: A Sourcebook* (New York: Oxford University Press, 2002).
Moaddel, Mansour, and Kamran Talatoff, eds., *Modernist and Fundamentalist Debates in Islam: A Reader* (New York: Palgrave MacMillan, 2002).
Norton, Augustus Richard, ed., *Civil Society in the Middle East*, 2 vols. (Leiden: Brill, 1995–1996, 2005).
Rahman, Fazlur, *Islam and Modernity: Transformation of an Intellectual Heritage* (Chicago: University of Chicago Press, 1982, latest ed. reprint n.d.).
Saeed, Javaid, *Islam and Modernization: A Comparative Analysis of Pakistan, Egypt, and Turkey* (Westport, CT: Praeger, 1994).
Salvatore, Armando, *Islam and the Political Discourse of Modernity* (Berkshire, U.K.: Ithaca Press, 1999, new ed. 2000).

Non-Western Culture and Development Theory

Barr, Michael D., *Cultural Politics and Asian Values: The Tepid War* (London: Routledge, 2002).
Binder, Leonard, *Islamic Liberalism: A Critique of Development Ideologies* (Chicago: University of Chicago Press, 1988).
Kuran, Timur, *Islam and Mammon: The Economic Predicaments of Islamism* (Princeton: Princeton University Press, 2004).
Lee, Robert D., Jr., *Overcoming Tradition and Modernity: The Search for Islamic Authenticity* (Boulder: Westview Press, 1997).
Majid, Anouar, *Freedom and Orthodoxy: Islam and Difference in the Post Andalusian Age* (Stanford, CA: Stanford University Press, 2003).
Meijer, Roel, *Cosmopolitanism, Identity, and Authenticity in the Middle East* (Richmond, Surrey, U.K.: Curzon Press, 1999).
Migdal, Joel S., et al., eds., *State Power and Social Forces: Domination and Transformation in the Third World* (Cambridge, U.K.: Cambridge University Press, 1994).
Sadeq, Abul Hasan M., ed., *Development Issues in Islam* (Kuala Lumpur: International Islamic University of Malaysia, 2006).
Schech, Susanne, and Jane Haggis, *Culture and Development: A Critical Introduction* (Oxford: Blackwell Publishers, 2000, latest ed. reprint 2003).
Wei-ming, Tu, ed., *Confucian Traditions in East Asian Modernity: Moral Education and Economic Culture in Japan and the Four Mini-Dragons* (Cambridge, MA: Harvard University Press, 1996).
Zhang, Wei-Bin, *Confucianism and Modernization: Industrialization and Democratization of the Confucian Regions* (New York: St. Martin's Press, 1999).

Index

About the Author

JOHN W. JANDORA is Supervisory Analyst with the U.S. Army Special Operations Command. He retired from the U.S. Marine Corps Reserve at the rank of Colonel as a veteran of the Vietnam and Gulf Wars. He is Adjunct Professor of International Relations at Webster University, Fort Bragg–Pope Air Force Base, and a frequent lecturer at U.S. military schools, including the Command and General Staff College. He was twice deployed to Baghdad as Senior Advisor in an Iraqi national security project and served as Senior Advisor to the military and technical schools of the Saudi Arabian National Guard. He is the author of *Militarism in Arab Society: An Historiographical and Bibliographical Sourcebook* (Greenwood Press, 1997), *Saudi Arabia: Cultural Behavior Handbook*, and *The March from Medina: A Revisionist Study of the Arab Conquests*. He received his Ph.D. in Near Eastern History from the University of Chicago.